THE BERMUDA TRIANGLE

by

Adi-Kent Thomas Jeffrey

WARNER
PAPERBACK
LIBRARY

A Warner Communications Company

D0057259

WARNER PAPERBACK LIBRARY EDITION
First Printing: June, 1975

This Warner Paperback Library Edition is published by arrangement with New Hope Publishing Company, Inc.

Cover design by Gene Light

Cover photos by Dave Porter

Map and back cover art by Walter Hortens

Photograph section compiled and designed by Thomas Nozkowski

Warner Paperback Library is a division of Warner Books, Inc., 75 Rockefeller Plaza, New York, N.Y. 10019.

A Warner Communications Company

Printed in the United States of America

Not associated with Warner Press, Inc. of Anderson, Indiana

ACKNOWLEDGEMENTS

My heartfelt thanks to the countless librarians, editors, historic societies, universities, staff members of magazines, newspapers, governmental and military departments both here and abroad who aided me so graciously in this work.

What I owe also to a score of devoted friends who went far beyond the call of brotherhood in their assistance to me, as well as to the many individuals who so kindly shared their experiences with me, truly cannot be put into words.

Most special and profound gratitude to Phyllis and Stanley Pogran; to Min and Bob Hilton; and to my husband and daughter, all precious people without whose advice and encouragement this book would not exist.

*To Bobby who flew all the storied winds
of the world and, no doubt, still does.*

Nothing in life is to be feared.
It is only to be understood.
                    Marie Curie

INTRODUCTION

The puzzle now referred to as the "Bermuda Triangle" must be the most intriguing bafflement on the face of the globe. It certainly seems that way when one gazes intently at the aging tapestry of the area's history and tries to follow all the fascinating threads that weave in and out to form the design.

The picture as a whole is bright and sunny. It is just that there are some faint-hued strands of incidents that comprise the mist in the background and the shadows on the wall that, though they are scarcely discernible without study, they are there and they are important. They command attention after a time for the very reason they do not command it at first; they are soft-hued and delicate. But, ah, how they create an effect! Once one detects their presence, one cannot conceive of the whole picture without them. It would be a glaring, unprovocative and uninteresting tapestry, indeed, that had no shadings . . . no darkness here and there for depth, pulling the eye back—back—and stirring the mind into wondering: what lies behind the colorful figures, the pastel walls, the green water?

Studied as such, the Triangle Mystery is a challenge to us. Man is ever urging forward in trying to unravel the Unknown. And if there is something to be uncovered and discovered, he will find it out. He always has. And he loves the searching of the shadows.

But to shrink from the mystery, as primitive man did before an eclipse out of needless and useless fear, is to fall into folklore fright and the stagnancy of superstition. Instead, an examination into the Triangle Mystery should stimulate curiosity and investigation.

And remember, from a viewpoint of pure mathematical percentages, the tragedies in the Triangle area are minuscule. If one wants to worry about statistics, worry about the number of drunken drivers on the highways and drug addicts in the back alleys, not the Bermuda Triangle.

Though sad events have occurred in this zone and the experiences of many unfortunates in this area over the centuries comprise the substance of this book, one must keep in mind the incidents form such a minor percentage as to be negligible. Millions have voyaged safely and joyously by ship and plane to Bermuda, the Bahamas, Haiti and Puerto Rico as well as to every other part of the globe.

So to forego a trip in any zone because of the Bermuda Triangle Mystery is to lend power to something that may, in the long run, be proven to have no power other than what we give it by our own fears.

In any case, there is nothing to be afraid of. If there is some effect being manifested in this area, then man will discover it and how to cope with it. That takes study not stupefaction. Fear magnifies a problem; understanding diminishes it. This book is intended to stir up inquiry and answers; not panic and pandemonium.

So go ahead and fly to Bermuda or the Caribbean's lush isles or wherever and enjoy yourself. I have no doubts that everyone can and will do this. Just recently my faith in man's basic sureness in the security of his being was thoroughly grounded after a conversation with a young friend of mine, Kim Hogstrom, who graduated from high school this past June.

I asked Kim what she planned to do now that she was launching forth into life. She thought for a moment. My thoughts raced through her possible aspirations: college? airline stewardess? nursing? secretary?

Her answer was not long in coming.

"I want to sail into the Bermuda Triangle!"

Dare any of us be less curious and confident?

CONTENTS

THE BERMUDA TRIANGLE

Chapter One

Bermuda is a place so terrible to all that ever touched on them.

1609 Journal of William Strachey
Secretary of Virginia Colony

WHAT IS THE
BERMUDA TRIANGLE?

What is the Bermuda Triangle?

This is a question one hears more and more. It pops up on television specials, radio talk shows and in magazines, newspapers and books. In fact, today it seems to be surfacing everywhere.

What is it?

Simply put: the Bermuda Triangle is a mystery zone where thousands of men and hundreds of ships and planes have been disappearing for years without a trace and utterly without explanation.

No one can say for sure just where the catchy name came from, but it is believed to hark back to a newspaper report in the 1940's which described the flight pattern of a group of lost planes in that area as "triangular."

In any case, though the term "Bermuda Triangle" may be of fairly recent vintage, its mystery is not. It has been a zone of disaster that has plagued man since the earliest days of seafaring in the New World. Then, as now, lovely lime-toned waters lapped the shores of the Bermuda Islands, the southern coast of North America and on down to Cuba, Haiti and Puerto Rico, all with seeming innocence, but—

Is there something unknown lurking in that region?

Centuries ago, man said that there was. Some of the New World's oldest navigational records refer to the island of Bermuda as the "Isles of the Devils."

Columbus was the first known voyager to the area and he experienced several weird incidents. He and his men saw "a remarkable ball of fire" fall into the sea on one occasion while sailing through these strange waters. He also reported that his men were terrified by a baffling disturbance of the ship's compass in that region. So an air of mystery was given this Bermuda Zone by its first known navigator.

There are over 300 coral islands in this part of the Atlantic. Only a handful of them—some 20—are inhabited even to this day. Around 400 years ago, no one wanted to go near them much less live on one, for the "Devils' Islands" formed the core of a whole body of superstitions that created such a fear of that area, it was avoided by seafarers more than any other place on earth. Fearful and mysterious demons of the dark lurked there in the waters' depths.

Now, nearly five centuries after Columbus, the question is being raised again: *is* there something unknown existent in that region? If not demons or devils, some strange and inexplicable force?

Man is beginning to think that there is. He is wondering if within that guileless green bordered by Bermuda, the southern coast of the United States and the West Indies, (and *over* it and *under* it) there might not lie hidden some power that annihilates all that comes inside its boundaries at certain times and under certain circumstances.

A lot of investigators all over the world, both scientific and unscientific, are pondering the problem.

England was deliberating it some 300 years ago. As early as the late 1600's, Lloyd's of London, the great insurance company, already established as the nerve-center of British shipping, made noises about it. Losses in that mid-Atlantic area were tremendous, far exceeding those in other parts of the globe.

In an age of piracy and open privateering amongst navies of many nations, all greeding to get the other man's gold, this was not too surprising. The Bermuda and West Indies waters lay in the line of the Spanish armada route that toted back annual shiploads of gold, silver, spices, slaves and other precious commodities from Mexico and South America to Spain. So it was natural that losses due to pirating attacks as well as autumn storms were the order of the day. From such obvious causes over 300 known treasure ships still lie buried in the seas off Bermuda awaiting unearthing.

But was there something more than pirates and storms to deal with in that watery region?

Suspicion lurked long after the bejeweled isles had been discovered by the Spanish explorer, Juan de Bermudez, in 1515. No one wanted any part of them. In fact, if it hadn't been for a storm wrecking the English ship, the *Sea Venture*, on the shoals of Bermuda nearly a century later, the coral-reefed island would probably not have been colonized for many years to follow.

The *Sea Venture* was bearing settlers to the

new founded colony of Virginia in July of 1609. About 150 of them. But once in the Danger Zone a storm of tremendous proportions slammed the vessel around until even the stout-hearted expedition leader, Sir George Somers, was waxing discouraged. Refusing to show his fears to his crew or passengers, he kept the men pumping and bailing for four days. Finally, just as he feared there could be no further possibility of keeping the ship afloat, he spied the island of Bermuda. Fortunately, a wedge-shaped reef clutched the distressed vessel in its grasp and held it there until every man aboard was safely landed ashore and all necessary equipment was salvaged.

Then after its obliging wait, the stricken ship lurched out of its berth and sank with a groan. A long sleep awaited it. It was not disturbed until 1958 when a diver, Edmund Downing of Virginia along with Teddy Tucker of Bermuda, explored the bony ribs of the near-ancient vessel buried in the sea bottom off Fort Saint Catherine.

The shipwrecked crew and passengers were forced to make a life for themselves on the island for nine months before an escape was able to be effected. But it was not the tearful task they all thought it would be. They found shelters easy to manufacture from the abundance of growth on the isle and food was all around them. From the first day, they were able to gather tasty fish, lobster, crabs and turtles from the sandy coves.

It was not long before the reluctant settlers were not so reluctant. They found the wild hog meat, the cool fruits and the mild air a joy beyond anything they'd known in England or could expect in Virginia.

With all this good public relations, it is not difficult to understand how the lovely coral-reefed island would, within three years, become a colony of Great Britain.

Later it got a bonus in advertising which it didn't anticipate from a playwright named William Shakespeare. He used the wreck of the *Sea Venture*, as the basis for his play, *The Tempest*.

And it's thanks to the journal of an observing passenger aboard the *Venture* that he was able to do so. That man was William Strachey, Secretary-elect of Virginia colony.

Strachey along with Sir George Somers, the expedition leader and his partner, Sir Gates, and the ship's Captain Newport, were the only persons among the total of 150 that knew a dreadful secret.

The idyllic spot upon which they had landed was none other than one of the fearful "Isles of the Devils!"

They decided not to divulge the awful truth to the rest of the passengers. But Somers confided it to his journal. He must have been pleasantly surprised when he first set foot on the sandy soil to find nothing more terrifying in the lush brush than a startled wild island hog.

As for the innocent others—they set happily about making huts for themselves out of palmetto leaves and cedar posts while Somers scrawled nervously in his diary that they were all destined to dwell at a place "terrible to all that touched upon it."

But Bermuda's area oddities never were related to devils in the brush or demons in the depths but to something much less mythological though, perhaps, just as mystical.

Somers wrote about one such eerie circumstance that occurred on a night during the voyage soon after the *Venture* first entered the Danger Zone.

The expedition leader was standing watch. He leaned back against the oak railing of the quarter deck and stared around in the dense blackness. At night when the rise and fall of huge swells lifted a ship into stark nothingness of air one moment and plunged it down into the inky depths of sea the next, one felt the greatest awe of existence, he was sure. He listened passively to the groan of ropes and spars.

Suddenly, something caught the nobleman's eye. Something dazzling. Far brighter than the diffused glow of a whale oil lantern, a light shone brilliantly into his upturned gaze.

Sir George Somers watched in fascination. It moved like a Thing alive from shroud to shroud. Then it shot like a fiery blaze up the mainmast, hovered there about half way up; then dimmed to a flickering star-like form. On; then off. After a moment of complete darkness, as he stared, the light rekindled and appeared to leap overhead like no phenomenon of heaven or earth he'd ever seen before.

Strachey described the incident in his journal. Sir George's "apparition" made immortality in its pages. Shakespeare evidently made good use of the tale. He put the strange light to good effect in the personification of the spirit Ariel in *The Tempest*.

In the form of a dancing flame, Ariel boasts how he "boarded the King's ship, now on the

beak, now in the waist, the deck, in every cabin
. . . flamed amazement."

But the dancing light was not the last mystery
to be recorded by Strachey. The Bermuda Danger Zone chalked up within his pages the earliest
vanishing of a rescue vessel: the boat that set
out from Bermuda to go for help.

It was a longboat salvaged from the *Venture*.
Under the command of Mate Henry Ravens, the
sturdy little craft was prepared for the long
voyage. Sailors heaved kegs of precious fresh
water, wine and crudely woven baskets filled
with fruits, nuts and sea turtles for meat. What
remained of the ship's instruments were placed
aboard and a stout though small canvas sail was
spread to the wind. On August 28th, just a
month after the wreck, the new *Venture* set sail
from the Bermuda shore. Mate Ravens had with
him a volunteer crew of seven men.

With hearts full of uncertainties and the air
ringing with cries of "fare-ye-well," the remaining colonists stood on the sand and watched
the brave longboat sail briskly out to sea.

The settlers walked slowly back to their palmetto huts. It was not an unhappy circumstance
being wrecked where they were. All the same,
they thought the rest of the world should at
least know where they were. Friends and rela-
tives were on the other ships in the original
fleet that had set out for Virginia. They yearned
to have them know they were safe and sound.
And in the long run, who did not wish to be
saved and return to those who were their own?

Two nights later, the new colonists of the isle
were startled to see a small craft blowing towards them from the horizon.

It couldn't be—

It was. The longboat was back.

Ravens somewhat chagrined, had to admit the tiny expeditionary force had not gotten under way yet. It could not find its way out of the reefs for even a start towards Virginia.

On the following Friday, September 1st, the rescue squad prepared again. Amidst the same flurry of excitement and good cheers, the longboat set sail once again.

With a smile of confidence on his brown face, Mate Ravens lifted one hand in a farewell salute.

"Fear ye not," he told the small band of watchers on the shore. "Ye shall be saved. We shall return during the next moon!"

When the next moon came, the eager islanders gathered brush and dried sticks all afternoon, placing them in bonfire position on the highest sand knoll overlooking the sea. From time to time, one of them would pause and stare into the azure waters reaching far away towards emptiness. There wasn't the sign of a prow or a sail.

Yet hopes were high. The weather had been balmy from the very day the longboat had departed. Surely in the hands of such skilled seamen they had made it, had been welcomed at the Virginia colony and were even now leading a rescue ship towards their isle.

But the shadows fell over the sea-licked sandy stretches and not so much as a winged gull landed on the powdery beaches. All that night the bonfires were kept blazing atop the knoll to guide Ravens and his rescuers in. As dawn lighted up the darkest coves and the deepest dells of forest brush, the marooned settlers finally shook their heads and swallowed their disappointments. No one was coming. Ravens had not returned.

He never did. They never saw Henry Ravens or any of his crew of seven again. The longboat and its would-be life-savers vanished in the turquoise sea without a clue as to what their fate had been. It's not known to this day. Not so much as a plank of wood from the longboat or fragment of its sail or a pocket from a seaman's coat ever floated to any shore anywhere.

To men of the 17th century, the demons of the deep had dragged the men down to their underwater lair. To thoughtful men of today, it was the first unsolved vanishing ever recorded for the Bermuda Triangle Danger Zone.

To the stranded colonists at Bermuda, it meant eight more months of waiting and planning. Eventually, they managed to build two seaworthy boats from the material at hand, large enough to accommodate them all. In them a second expedition set sail for Virginia. This time it was successful. The stout-timbered ships sailed from Bermuda on May 10, 1610, almost a full year from the day of shipwreck. They arrived at Jamestown 580 miles away in exactly two weeks time, bringing to an end the first and longest adventure in the waters of the "Isles of the Devils."

Just what and where such devils might be lurking, only Henry Ravens and seven men might have learned. But they were gone into some unknown world from where no man ever looked back and out of which no man ever spoke.

So the mystery of the vanished longboat remained and haunted the New World settlers for a long time.

It was only the beginning of a puzzle that would last for centuries.

Chapter Two

The galleons and fleet usually leying at Habana and the whole Spanish armada sails for Spain by this line.

Words written on an old map dated in the 16th century. They follow a line traced from the northern end of Cuba close to Key West which then veers northeast. A close delineation of the western border of the Bermuda Triangle!

DANGER-FRAUGHT PASSAGE
OF THE ARMADAS

If the *Sea Venture's* unexpected landing at Bermuda brought the area a fresh and promising publicity, it stood alone in that claim. The majority of ships pressing through the winds and waves of those far-away seas found more troubles and treachery than tropical delights.

And even the most ignorant and superstitious knew better than to attribute these problems to devils or demons.

Unless one wanted to call Spain a devil of avarice and aggression . . . and all the other nations left sitting by the hearth to cool their heels and lick their wounded egos, her pursuing demons.

The opening of the New World to Spain through the discoveries by Christopher Columbus in the late 1400's of the West Indes Islands, coincided with victorious military achievements at home. Under the rule of Ferdinand and Isabella the king's forces feverishly and finally drove the troublesome Moors out of their kingdom. For the first time in centuries Spain could turn her attention to uniting her people and developing her powers.

What better direction to look than the New

World for fresh and rich resources to fill the treasury depleted by long years of armed conflict?

Spain was intent upon building the strongest army and navy in Europe. The wherewithall to do this was obviously inherent in Columbus' island discoveries and subsequently of Central America. There would be wider reaches in the future, she knew. That goal was not long in being reached. Spain's Fernandez de Cordoba landed on the coast of Mexico just 15 years after Columbus' last voyage.

Cordoba was followed a year later by Grijalva and within two years, Mexico's conquest was completed by Cortes, that most ardent conquistador. By the early 16th century, Spain had established an iron-boot foothold on much of the West Indes, Mexico and Peru. And she didn't intend to step off.

Not only had she discovered the eye-glazing delights of gold, silver and precious gems in these distant lands but an equally profitable resource in the form of slave labor. The gentle Arawak Indians of Central America were easily enslaved and the Spanish lost no time in clasping the chains in place. As the years wore on, Spain's slave trade rose in importance until it was second only to her plate fleets that carried the treasure of Mexico and South America to the home country.

Other countries in Europe awoke seething over the news of Spain's activities in the New World. They wanted in.

So to the Caribbean poured other nations' ships—British, French, Dutch, Portuguese, Danish and Swedish sailing through the blue-green waters, ignorant of the perils that lay embedded in shoals and reefs; hurricanes and whirlpools. They were only thinking of the riches to be had.

Slowly, various islands were grabbed; plantations were established; houses were built and land was cleared for cattle-raising and crop-growing.

But getting the little luxuries of life was another matter. Ships had to be too loaded with men, horses and arms to carry even necessities for comfortable living. Thus arose a whole new Caribbean "fleet": the smugglers' ships. So welcome was this breed of settler, hideouts for the illegal tradesmen grew to be as plentiful as plantations. There was scarcely a cove or coral cave where these "merchantmen" didn't gather to carry on business, obtain fresh water or careen their ships.

Such practices led to a robust illicit practice that engulfed the whole Caribbean for centuries —piracy. Buccaneering to be successful always needed three things: plenty of shipping to prey upon; a geographic location that supplied coves along a shoreline and lastly, a safe and sure market for its plunder.

The West Indies fulfilled every requirement and piracy held sway with fervor for centuries.

But by 1700 the breed of lawless thief of the seas vanished under the invasion of a lawful brand of pirate: the privateer. England, especially, flying high on wide wings of colonial and commercial expansion, needed protection against the ravages of piracy and the competition of Spanish conquests. The privateer was her answer.

Privately owned vessels received well-wishing commissions to act as men-of-war. They were licensed to seize and plunder enemy shipping and enemy settlements. The more the better.

This forced Spain to build greater and faster galleons and to sail them in convoy as a protective measure.

So the powerful once-a-year armadas crossed the Atlantic with a sharp "eye out" for privateer attacks and as well the quick-silver storms and deceiving, twisting currents and cross-currents. The armada's pattern was systematic.

Upon arrival, some of the ships headed for South America; the rest sailed for Mexico. After loading to the beams with treasure and slaves, the South American ships would meet at the Isthmus of Panama; then sail together for Havana, Spain's most important port in the New World. There this group came together with a second squadron bearing gold and silver from Mexico. From this point of convergence, the combined fleets set sail in one tightly-knit armada for the home trip.

Their course took them through the bottleneck of the Florida Straits and the Bahama Channel, passing Cayo Hueso, and on into the Gulf Stream riding northwards past Bermuda, headed for Hatteras on the Carolina coast.

The western boundaries of the Bermuda Danger Zone were the lifeline of Spanish trade. But sometimes and to some men and ships this route became a death-line.

The Spanish admirals did their best through this danger-beset passage but that was often not good enough. The galleons were top-heavy of construction and not the stoutest in seaworthiness. On many occasions when meeting a storm head-on, or running into precarious vortexes, the vessels keeled over and sank like parchment boats laden with rocks. There were many instances when entire fleets were scattered or sunk. In the 16th century, 41 treasure-filled ships went down; in the 17th century, 38 more followed into the green seas of that region.

And some ships lie we know not where, for they vanished into a mysterious place that denies them discovery even to this day.

Take, for example, the treasure-laden flota that set forth for the long trip home to Spain in the autumn of 1750. The fleet was under the command of Captain Don Juan Manuel de Bonilla. It consisted of five galleons all carrying the annual take of precious metals and gems from the Spanish possessions in the New World. The five rendezvoused as customary at Havana. Captain Bonilla commanded the flagship, a proud high-decked vessel called the *Nuestra Senora de Guadalupe*. Grandly, the *Guadalupe* led the convoy to sea. With sails arching to a spanking wind the galleons glided easily through the Florida Straits and into the Bahama Channel, riding the current of the Gulf Stream north.

As the flota approached Cape Hatteras where it was to veer eastwards across the Atlantic, the serene waters began to darken and churn. The sky overhead became the color of lead.

Captain Bonilla stood at the rail of the quarterdeck. His brows knit. He knew there was treachery in these parts, particularly in the autumn months. He was approaching the point that navigators considered the most dangerous stretch of coastline on the Atlantic ocean. A point where the northbound Gulf Stream ran head-on into the cold current of the Arctic, heaving sand and spray tower-high into the air on a stormy day.

Edging this turbulence were strands of narrow, sandy islands, a kind of outer banks of the British-owned Carolina shore. Bonilla knew that on these lived a hardy crew of men that made their living as smugglers and wreckers of storm-tossed vessels just such as his.

He ran an uneasy finger under his high braided collar. Peace had just been declared between England and Spain by the signing of the Treaty of Aix but neither nation felt it was a secure peace. Largely due to Spain, Bonilla had to admit.

In less than six weeks after the date set for armaments to be put aside between the two countries, a Spanish squadron had loomed over the horizon and made straight for the Carolina coast. It sailed swiftly up the Cape Fear River and before anyone could reason why it was there, it wiped out the English settlement of Brunswick, burning the houses, killing the residents and looting the properties, carrying away all valuables including a shipload of slaves.

As if this were not enough, Spain's vessels had the continual bad habit of landing on the Carolina outer islands and stealing their cattle and hogs.

Captain Bonilla swallowed hard now and leaned over the rail. He could plainly see the waves crashing on the restless sands of the finger-thin strips of land.

He raised his brass spy-glass, swept it leeward, then swung it forward towards the increasingly heaving sea.

The captain sent for his lieutenant.

The young officer bent against the wind.

"It blows foul, señor, I was once in a hurricane in the East Indies and the beginning of it had much the same appearance as this. So be sure we have plenty of sea room," ordered Bonilla.

"Si, Capitán. It has a very ugly look. I fear we are going to have a fierce gale of wind."

They did. By eight o'clock that night, the hurricane struck with full force. Captain Bonilla, expectant of what the consequences might be, should the wind shift direction suddenly, placed the carpenters by the mainmast with broad-axes. He knew from experience that at the moment one may want to cut it away to save the ship, an axe may not be found.

As the ship groaned and whined in every timber, the captain shouted his orders and the crew worked diligently.

The hapless *Guadalupe* endured tenaciously, but the odds were too great for her. Every time she tried to rise and shake her decks free of the gigantic waves, they smashed her with repeated blows. The stout sails flew out of the gaskets that bound them to the yards. The staunch wooden hull began to rip open like a basket. The ship was being pounded to pieces.

Captain Bonilla lashed himself near the kicking wheel where four strong-armed quartermasters sweated as they tried to steer the dying galleon. He shouted to the elements:

"Madre Mia! To think the wind can have such power!"

Below, the lieutenant pitched in with the toiling gang manning the pumps.

Before long, one of the pumps choked and the water gained in the hold.

The young officer pushed his way to the deck. It was a heart-freezing sight to behold. A total darkness of pitching waves enveloped everything. The wind roared louder than thunder and interspersed was a kind of blue lightning he'd never seen the likes of before. The ship was much pressed, yet was doing all she could, shaking her sides and groaning at every stroke.

The lieutenant fought his way towards the captain lashed upon the deck to windward. He tied himself alongside of him.

"We must lower the yards, for the ship is much pressed Capitán," he shouted to Bonilla.

The captain shook his head as white-foamed fury splashed across his brown features.

"No, if we attempt that, señor, we shall lose them, for a man aloft can do nothing. Besides, their being down would ease the ship but little. The mainmast is a sprung mast. Would it could heave overboard without carrying everything with it—"

Just then, a sailor below deck lurched towards them, his frightened features washed by sea spray.

"The water has gained so, Capitán, we can no longer stand to the pumps!"

The lieutenant turned towards the captain.

"Shall we cut away, señor?"

"As speedily as you can!"

Accordingly, the young officer and the sailor pressed their way along the wind-and-wave swept deck, signalling the carpenters wildly. Within minutes the men were ready to bend their backs into the chains with pole-axes and cut away the lanyards when a violent wave broke square on board of them, carrying away everything that was left on the deck. With a loud roar, the main mast splintered and crashed to the boards.

The galleon heaved and nearly went over on her beam ends. Slowly she righted herself.

"Gracias a Diós!" murmured Bonilla as he realized how close their escape had come to be.

Gradually, the winds diminished and the storm abated.

With the coming of dawn, the sailors were crossing themselves in gratitude. The *Guadalupe* had made it!

On a gust of wind, the stricken vessel limped wearily into the mouth of the Ocracoke River. Like it or not, and as things were, Captain Bonilla felt he did like it, the valiant vessel was coming to berth at shores somewhat less than sympathetic but solid land nonetheless. With a cargo valued at a million pieces of eight!

Captain Bonilla picked up his spy-glass and scanned the sea. There was no sight of any of the other four galleons.

One had been close to his leeward side during the early stages of the storm. He'd spied it for a brief time before the winds, rain and the mountainous waves had blotted out all visual ability.

The other three he had not seen since the onslaught of the hurricane.

The vessel Bonilla had seen, he soon learned, had survived also . . . thanks to the wreckers or "bankers" of the shore islands. Some of the crew had been saved and taken into Norfolk from whence they were shipped, (along with the 32,000 pieces of eight she was carrying) to England.

Bonilla and his crew were treated with cautious hospitality by Governor Johnston of Carolina colony. It was a sensitive international situation, but the two sides eventually weathered the friction.

After a long, itchy, uncertain month filled

with everything from mutiny to trouble with the local customs and seizure laws, Bonilla was released and returned to Spain.

Before departing the shores of Carolina, the Spaniard tried to unearth some news of the other three galleons in his flota. There was nothing to be discovered. The last sighted of the ships was at Currituck Inlet and Topsail Inlet. Then nothing more was seen of them.

There was no word even from the "bankers" who must surely, if anyone could, know of the whereabouts of the valuable cargo carried by the Spanish ships. But history doesn't record one confirmation of what and where the galleons went down. It is a mystery that they could have so completely vanished in an area where islanders spent their lives watching and saving. A fortune in gold, silver, cocoa, balsam and a rare red dye called cochineal, vanished along with their vessels right within sight of the Carolina Banks.

The islanders searched relentlessly but were never able to find a trace of any of the missing three galleons. Nor did any bodies wash ashore. Nor did a fragment of clothing, nor so much as a single piece of silver or of gold ever come to light. Neither a single barrel of balsam or cocoa. The three vessels simply vanished along with every splinter of yardarm and rail and keg of cargo.

To the expert wreckers of the Outer Banks, it was a mystery they tried hard to solve. Wrecking was a fine art and they'd refined it. But in the case of the lost ships of the armada in that year of 1750, their skills came to naught.

They never could find a sliver of wood much

less any treasure from the three galleons that vanished without a trace in a corner of that historic Danger Zone.

Chapter Three

Authentic accounts from Bermuda and Nassau . . . have . . . forced upon me the dreadful conviction that there is no hope.

From a letter written by Governor Joseph Alston, husband of Theodosia Burr, to his father-in-law, Aaron Burr, in February of 1813.

A LADY VANISHES

The remarkable loss of three Spanish galleons off the Atlantic shore line without a remnant or clue as to their whereabouts was only the beginning of a noticeable mystery in that stretch of ocean bordering the southern coast of what became the United States of America.

Sixty-two years later, the insidious watery region made an historic imprint. It obliterated a slim, fast-paced packet ship that was heading north from South Carolina to New York City, leaving not the smallest tell-tale sign of what its destiny had been.

The tragedy made history books because its chief passenger was the daughter of a former Vice-President of the United States, Aaron Burr. She was Theodosia Burr Alston, wife of Governor Joseph Alston of South Carolina.

Theodosia seems to have been one of those beauties of the world whose charms were constantly being outweighed by tragedies in the balance of mortal existence. She had lost her mother at a young age, married at seventeen and was forced to make a life far from the home and the father she loved so much . . . a love that was to be tried and found true through the

most difficult testing times—those years following Aaron Burr's loudly declaimed and fatal
duel with Alexander Hamilton. Even though
Vice President of the United States, he was
forced into hiding because of a warrant issued
for his arrest on the charge of murder.

Through months of running and subsequent
stormy days of trial for treason, the vibrant Burr
was acquitted by the courts—but public outrage
was not satisfied. Burr felt for the sake of peace
and future, he had no choice but to flee his
country.

The years of exile were another heartbreak
for Theodosia. Her son, she bemoaned, had to
grow up with no knowledge of his grandpa who
was, in her eyes, the genius of his day; the true
keeper of her heart.

But lightness burst on her soul like a spring
morning when a letter came from her father in
England saying that he was coming home. After
four years, he was coming back to New York!
What joy!

The celebrant mood was shortlived. Her
young son contracted the dreaded malarial fever
while vacationing at the Alston's summer resi-
dence on Pawley's Island. Refused permission
to employ the current treatment of dosing,
nothing could the doctors think of to do to save
the child of the First Family of the state. It is
unlikely any kind of medication known then
could have saved him. Ten year old Aaron Burr
Alston died on the last day of June in 1812.

Grief-stricken, Theodosia could only write out
her heart's sorrow to her father just recently
established in New York City as a practicing
attorney.

". . . I have lost my boy," she wrote, "My child

is gone forever . . . May Heaven, by other blessings, make you some amends for the noble grandson you have lost."

Plunged into sorrow and illness, Theodosia could not cope with living any longer in a climate that bothered her constantly with its heat and humidity. She was ill of body and soul with the loss of her son and now superseded on that, fear for her father's future.

Finally, knowing how she pined to see her father again, Joseph Alston was persuaded that a change of air and scenery might put life back into the limbo Theodosia was creating about herself. He decided to send her up to New York to stay with her father for a time. He started arrangements to charter a vessel especially for his wife's voyage. Before he could complete his plans, a New Yorker arrived at his plantation, "The Oaks," in Charleston and introduced himself. He was Timothy Green, confidante and friend of Aaron Burr. The attorney had requested him to make the journey to South Carolina and personally escort the fragile Theodosia northwards.

There was not much Alston could do, though he felt it a slight to have a special escort sent from New York. He acquiesced to Green's arrangements which had already been concluded prior to his arrival. They included passage on a packet ship called the *Patriot*.

The *Patriot*, known for its speed, customarily carried mail and freight from coastal port to coastal port. But since the outbreak of war with England, the speedy craft had been used as a privateer, nettling British shipping.

For this particular occasion, in deference to the distinguished nature of its mission, bearing the First Lady of South Carolina, the packet dismounted its guns and stored them under deck. In addition, permission was obtained from the British blockade forces to grant passage to the *Patriot* when it approached the New York harbor. The English had readily complied with the request.

As a further role in its peaceful mission, the packet was carrying freight not arms to the northern port: a goodly load of Governor Alston's renowned golden grain. It was the famous Alston rice pounded into grain form and it was to be sold in New York as a form of financing Theodosia's trip. It would seem even governors had to search for extra dollars during a hardship wartime era!

The day set for the voyage was December 31st, the last day of a fateful year—1812. Governor Joseph Alston made sure a guardian of his own entered the picture. He asked his uncle, William Algernon Alston, to escort his wife and her party to the point of departure and see them safely off.

Accordingly, Mr. Alston was on hand early in the morning prior to departure day. It was a brisk December day, a coach and two ready to bear the assembled group on its way to the harbor at Georgetown on Winyah Bay. The party consisted of Theodosia, her personal physician and her maid in addition to the dutiful escort, Timothy Green.

The Governor stood for a long moment on the curve of driveway before his mansion, watching the coach sputter down the lane and fade into the distant green of great moss-dripping oaks. He thought for a moment of the last swift image he had caught of his lovely wife, smiling at him from behind the carriage window as it pulled away from him. Her dark hair peeking out from beneath the crisp mourning bonnet, framed such a graceful oval of features. In that pale face gazed out the deepest, darkest eyes he'd ever seen. They seemed ever to glow with a penetrating inner light; they always had to him ever since he'd first met her on a visit to New York, when he was only twenty-two and she was seventeen.

Now she was twenty-nine, a woman whose sorrows showed in her complete fragility, which was, in itself, a difficult-to-grasp contradiction in her personality. No woman in that day could compare with Theodosia Burr Alston for strength and keenness of mind, sharpness of wit and thoroughly-studied knowledge.

Joseph Alston turned and took one quick appraising glance at the depth and breadth of his rice plantation reaching outwards from where he stood for miles and miles.

He sighed. "The Oaks" would be utterly empty without Theo; hollow and without purpose now for he knew not how long.

The Chief Executive of South Carolina had been trying the past six months to forget the memories of young Aaron. But he couldn't. He could still see the boy running down the wide staircase or galloping at his side along the plantation lanes or listening at his mother's feet by the hearth as she read to him from the classics.

Now he would have further memories to subdue for a while: his beloved wife sitting opposite him at the table, her face glowing over the shining damask, every ivory feature candle-lit and shimmering with shadows and sparks.

No more. Not for a long while now, he

thought as he listened to the ringing of his own booted feet across the polished hallway. He paused at the doorway to the peaceful parlor. Its emptiness tightened the coldness in his heart. For a moment he regretted having made no protest over the plans for a visit. But he also realized it would have done no good. Joseph Alston had long since learned to share his wife's love with a man there was no fighting. Father and daughter had a bond not even the most devoted husband could sever. Nor did he wish to. Whatever made Theo happy, made him happy. He had always left it that way.

The following day, Theodosia was feeling a happiness that she had not known in a long time. She leaned forward as the carriage came to a slow halt at the Georgetown dockside. The *Patriot* heaved slowly up and down at her moorings in the gently ruffling bay water. She could feel the slow excitement rising inside her. Here was the swift angelic messenger that was to bear her homewards back to her own city— back to her father. She put one foot out on the carriage step as she let her light weight rest on the arm of Timothy Green.

"Oh, it's beautiful! Beautiful to behold, is it not, Mr. Green? Soon we shall be wafting into the harbor I knew so well as a child. Oh, I cannot wait!"

Theodosia's maid smiled as she bent over the carriage seat and filled her arms with cloaks and hat boxes. Timothy Green picked up a portman- teau the driver had just rested at his feet and, guiding Theodosia by the elbow, steered her gently towards the ship's gangwalk.

Seeing the sudden pink in Mrs. Alston's face, her physician kept pace beside her on the other side, cautioning her against too much excitement.

"Oh, tosh!, good Doctor, I'm feeling alive again . . just a little!"

The *Patriot's* commander, Captain Overstocks, saluted smartly as the group made its way on board.

Timothy Green nodded his head in acknowledgement. The captain, he knew from investigation, was a most experienced and able pilot. There was no finer sailing master to be had along the Atlantic coast. Green felt satisfied that the Alston party was in safe hands. He made a final check with the contents of his greatcoat pocket. It was there. The message written in Governor Alston's own hand noting the special permission granted by the British authorities to permit passage of the pilot boat past the British warships.

The trip was scheduled to take five days. Probably they would be intercepted by the English ships at several points along the way. But no matter, there would be naught to fear from the blockade.

The weather was fair and the wind moderate. Captain Overstocks ordered "anchors aweigh" and in minutes the little ship was gliding swiftly out to sea and was on its way.

It was never seen again.

In vain, Aaron Burr walked the Battery along the New York waterfront, awaiting arrival of the packet. It never came. He was not to see his beloved Theodosia ever again.

Weeks went by and, finally, both the father and the husband in a mad exchange of communications, were forced to accept a horrible and unthinkable tragic conclusion: Theodosia and all those with her, had somehow, for some reason no one could trace, completely vanished at sea and would never be found.

In February of 1813, Joseph Alston wrote the heartbreak letter of his life to Aaron Burr:

"Your letter of the 10th, my friend, is received. This assurance of my fate is not wanting. . . . My boy—my wife—gone, both! This, then is the end of all hope we had formed. You may well observe that you feel severed from the human race. She was the last tie that bound us to the species. What have we left? . . . You are the only person in the world with whom I can commune on this subject; for you are the only person whose feelings can have any community with mine. You knew those we loved. Here, none know them; none valued them as they deserved. The talents of my boy, his rare elevation of character, his already extensive reputation for so early an age, made his death regretted by the pride of my family; but though certain of the loss of my not less admirable wife, they seem to consider it like the loss of an ordinary woman. Alas, they knew nothing of my heart. They have never known anything of it. After all, he is a poor actor who cannot sustain his little hour upon the stage, be his part what it may. But the man who was deemed worthy of the heart of *Theodosia Burr*, and who has felt what it was to be blessed with such a woman, will never forget his elevation."

Governor Alston never overcame his grief. He pined away and was dead in only three years' time. Aaron Burr kept to the stage boards almost another quarter of a century before his part was done. But not once during those long years to follow was Burr able to learn a hint of what had happened to the *Patriot*.

Thousands of words and dozens of explanations have been put forth over the century and a half that followed the strange disappearance of Theodosia Burr Alston. Not one theory has ever proven itself.

What could have happened?

Did the vessel hit into a storm? This was the most immediate thought but was abandoned as unlikely when not a speck of wreckage from the packet was ever picked up, as is invariably the case, even in the aftermath of the most destructive hurricane. Neither were any mortal remains or personal clothing ever sighted.

Was there sabotage since it was war time?

That theory, too, has been scrapped for there would have been telltale evidence of blown-up ship fragments floating on the sea's surface or washing up on the shoreline. There was nothing of the kind.

Did the vessel run into pirates?

This is a favorite solution and for years and years writers have been quoting final confessions of old reformed buccaneers about to depart this world. So many, however, recounted the facts in widely different descriptions, as they laid claim to the destruction of the unfortunate Theo, one finds the quantity of such death-bed confessions stretch credibility for the pirate theory.

However, the stories are fascinating and deserve attention.

The first one came to light in 1835. A tavern keeper in Mobile, Alabama, lay dying in his wretched room. The days brought him only torment as he would rise up weakly from time to time, gape first at one corner of the room; then the next, crying out each time:

"There she is! There she is!"

Finally, a Dr. Alex Jones was summoned by neighbors who heard the man groaning and shouting in near delirium. The doctor leaned over and took the man's pulse.

Grasping the physician's hand, the pale form on the bed muttered in anguish,

"She won't let me alone! She keeps coming back to haunt me! Make her go away!"

Dr. Jones looked quietly around, then back down at the patient's distraught face.

"Who? Make who go away?"

"Theodosia Burr!"

The doctor looked puzzled.

"Theodosia Burr! Why, she vanished at sea about a quarter of a century ago. What would you have to do with her?"

The man threw himself from side to side.

"I was one of the crew of a pirate ship that overran the ship she was on. We didn't know until after we'd capture her, who 't'was we had aboard. We divided the goods and drew lots to see who'd be the beauty's executioner—none of us lads wanted it . . but I drew the short straw. . . ."

The man gulped as though the terror of old had never left him.

"She begged me not to kill her—she did—Doctor. Oh what a lady she be! Told me who she be and how's she needed to get to New York to comfort her father in his adversity . . . but I couldn't listen. . . ."

The tavern keeper lifted himself up on one elbow with all the strength he could muster.

"I oughtn't a done it, Doctor, but I had no

choice, you see . . . 'n she walked that plank like a lady going out onto a ballroom floor. . . ."

The dying man dropped back on the mattress with a low groan.

"An' I see her walkin' that plank over 'n over . . . She keeps comin' towards me, her white arms outstretched . . Oh, Jesus save me. ."

Those were the last words from the tormented man who gasped when he had finished. He was dead. The doctor shook his head in wonder over the incident but told it frequently over the subsequent years.

It wasn't the last pirate declaration of guilt.

Another buccaneer hit the confession route on his death-bed. He was a Frenchman by the name of Jean Baptiste Callistre.

"I sailed with Monsieur Chauvet on the *Vengeance*. I was a gunner. One day we spied this little ship headed northwards and we gave easy chase, boarding her without a squabble. Found this gentlewoman of rare beauty in the cabin below deck. With our usual delight we tied her hands and feet and carried her over to the *Vengeance*. She was slim of form, but a fighter nonetheless. Well, we had our fun, as you can imagine, all the voyage back to our base on Galveston Island in the Gulf of Mexico.

"She didn't last the ordeal too well. Died, as I recall, a short time after our return to the island. Well, it was too bad. But c'est la vie. We buried her there near the old fort. Still lies ten feet down, I daresay . ."

At that point, the speaker produced, according to the account, a locket containing the ivory image of a young boy. On the golden case were inscribed the initials: T.A.

Some years after this aforementioned man

who seemed to be remarkably verbal at his final moment on earth, there came a confession from an aged man in Michigan, a Frank Burdick, who swore upon his death-bed that he was one of the pirates who had murdered Theodosia Burr in 1812.

This reformed corsair's confession fades into insignificance in comparison with the final sworn statement made by an ex-pirate four years later.

That man was, according to a magazine article written by Foster Haley in the magazine section of Charleston's *News and Courier* of February 15th, 1959, none other than the author of "Home Sweet Home," John Howard Payne!

The writer gives as his source "documents spaded up from the Archives Building of the State of Alabama in Montgomery" after 145 years of dust-collecting.

In these documents, John Howard Payne is purported to have declared during his final moments the truth about his ex-pirate days. He was a man without a country, far from his native land, dying in Tunis, Africa, a stronghold for pirates and plunderers. He wished to absolve his soul by an expiation of his past guilts.

Payne said he was the last surviving member of a pirate crew that roamed the Atlantic. His ship had captured the *Patriot*, he allegedly wrote, after a bloody one-sided battle that ended with a surrender by Captain Overstocks and what was left of the crew.

The pirates then murdered every one of them, including a woman who was obviously a noble-woman or lady of high birth. She was, he learned, Theodosia Burr.

Who she was meant little to the ruffians, declared Payne. She was blindfolded and forced to walk the plank just as were the others.

It was a deed that had preyed on his mind ever since and he had to tell about it at long last.

Distinguished a personage as was this last confessor, the most romantic and colorful version was yet to come. An account of the story appeared in the Charleston *News and Courier* of August 4th, 1963.

This article by R. J. Cannaday brings out a completely new angle: Theodosia kept a diary! In her journal, the astute woman kept a day by day account of all that happened to the *Patriot* and its crew and passengers. Before her afore-judged demise, she wrote down her last comments, sealed the document along with her wedding ring inside a bottle and threw it overboard.

That bottle was found a long time afterwards, washed ashore. The contents were subsequently purchased by a Colonel Justin Dane who showed them to his friends upon many an occasion.

Theodosia's alleged journal is purported to have described her voyage on the *Patriot* as thus:

"By six o'clock on the evening of their first day at sea, a wind of gale proportions arose and struck out smartly at the little craft. By dawn of the next day, a violent storm was in full swing."

Theodosia went up on deck. Captain Over-stocks was issuing orders to swing the ship east-wards. Soon they were pushing southward on the force of a terrific storm blowing to the south.

Finally, she noted the weather getting warmer; the ice around them was melting. The *Patriot*, explained the captain, had hit the Gulf

Stream. They were headed for Cuba and milder waters. There was nothing more to worry about.

Theodosia and her maid retired to rest.

But, apparently, peace was short-lived.

The next morning, seeing it was a serene and beautifully blue day, Theodosia arose early, completed her toilet before any of the other passengers were even awake and went up on the deck. Shading her eyes with one hand, she saw a ship in the distance.

Captain Overstocks studied it through his spy-glass.

He dropped it quickly and turned towards Theodosia with a startled look.

"The ship bears a black banner inscribed with a blood-red 'T'."

"So? That means what, sir?" asked Mrs. Alston.

"It means, madam, that we are about to come face to face with the most merciless and blood-thirsty pirate of all the notorious banditti in these waters—Captain Thaddeus Boncourt!"

What that face-to-face encounter entailed we, of course, could not know, for well in advance of the attack, Theodosia Alston tossed her account for posterity into the green Caribbean. According to this recounting of the incident, the last person to have had a close contact with the unfortunate Theodosia, was the Colonel Dane who came into possession of her wedding ring and diary. His hands were the first and, probably, the last to touch what the doomed First Lady of South Carolina had placed carefully into the safekeeping of the sea.

So goes the story. A colorful one, indeed.

Edward Rowe Snow, the noted New England writer and collector of sea lore, took painstaking time to trace a fascinating thread of Theodosia history. He then reported the interesting story of a woman's portrait found in a seashore hut of an old lady some years ago. The woman declared it had been given her by a sweetheart in her youth. He had been a wrecker and had come upon this painting which he presented to her. She in turn gave it to a doctor in payment for his services. Ultimately, the work of art came into the possession of a Glen Cove, New York art collector, a Mr. Herbert Lee Pratt. At his death in 1945, the main substance of his collection went to Amherst College, but his family kept the beautiful painting of the 19th century woman which has been declared to be a portrait of Theodosia Burr Alston by John Vanderlyn.

Another fascinating angle to one of the most puzzling incidents that ever occurred in America's history.

In spite of the long and probably continuing flow of explanations as to what the fate of Theodosia was, the truth remains, today, as before, a puzzle. No one has any real idea as to what actually happened to the swift little ship and its distinguished passenger. A fact that places the *Patriot's* disappearance well at the top of the long roster of unexplained vanishings in the Atlantic's Danger Zone.

A long list followed.

Chapter Four

Perhaps, in some mighty ocean Valhalla in amity and friendship, the heroes of the WASP meet together in the deep . . .

Revolutionary Fights and Fighters, 1900
by Cyrus Townsend Brady

THE U. S. NAVY
ENTERS THE MYSTERY

The War of 1812 served as backdrop for more than the mysterious disappearance of Theodosia Burr aboard a packet ship—it was the setting also for the vanishing of one of America's most formidable warships and its commander, a hero whose name was on everyone's lips.

His name was Johnston Blakeley.

The young naval officer was commissioned a master commandant in the U.S. Navy and given command of a ship in 1811. After the outbreak of hostilities with Great Britain, he was given command of a new warship, the *Wasp*. It was the all-out death blow dealt to an English brig-sloop, the *Reindeer*, one of England's most powerful fighters, by the *Wasp* in June of 1814 that spiralled the name of Johnston Blakeley to fame.

Then, without warning, in the fall of that same year, Captain Blakeley, his stalwart warship, and his entire crew simply slipped over the horizon and vanished from the sight of man forever.

No one—not the U.S. Navy, the foe herself, or the family of Blakeley—ever learned of a single clue that would aid in solving the mystery of what befell the victorious vessel . . . from that day to this.

Life began with drama for young Blakeley. When he was sailing from England with his family for America in 1782 as a child of one year old, his mother and a new baby brother died at sea just prior to docking at the South Carolina port of Charleston. Young Johnston had left his home land with a family of four. He arrived in the New World with only a father.

The Blakeleys stayed in Charleston for about a year, then moved to Wilmington where the father became established in a profitable mercantile business. By the time Johnston was grown to manhood, the elder Blakeley had amassed a sizeable fortune and he was able to send his son to the University of North Carolina at Chapel Hill in 1797. The youth's interests settled quickly on mathematics, navigation and surveying.

College was broken off when the elder Blakeley passed away and Johnston's inherited estate was reduced to nil by a fire that wiped out a small fortune. His guardian and long time family friend, Edward Jones, insisted he be responsible for the finishing of the boy's education, but the youth refused. He left the University and joined the United States Navy as a midshipman.

America's sea forces were practically a brand new institution. Only six years prior to that time, had the country been able to boast of a true navy. It had been on March 27, 1794 that Congress had taken sure steps to provide the United States with something resembling a real navy.

Such action was due to a president who was a strong advocate of efficient naval forces—he was

THE BERMUDA TRIANGLE

FOLD OUT MAP ⇶→

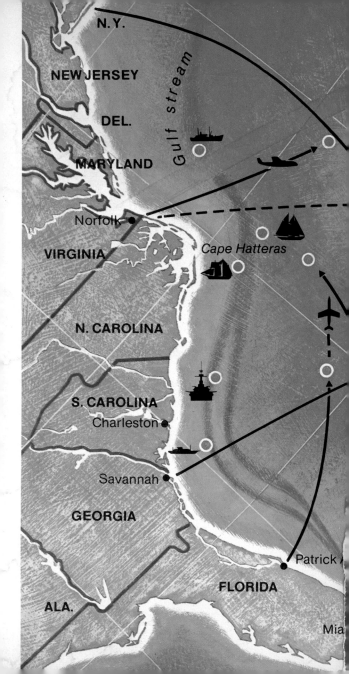

BERMUDA

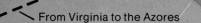

From Virginia to the Azores

En route to Kingston

From Barbados to Norfolk

BERMUDA TRIANGLE

From Key West

Returning
from Bimini

FB

NASSAU

BIMINI

From Isle of Pines
near Cuba

CUBA

ATLANTIC OCEAN

Puerto Rico Trench

PUERTO RICO

DOMINICAN REPUBLIC

HAITI

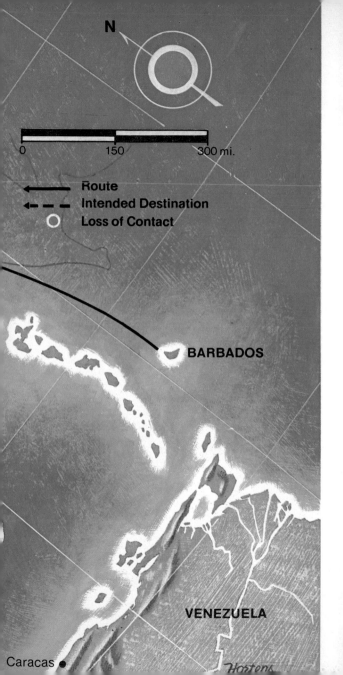

N

0   150   300 mi.

→ Route
⇠⇠ Intended Destination
◯ Loss of Contact

BARBADOS

VENEZUELA

Caracas ●

Hostens

Lost in the Bermuda Triangle

Ships	Year	Where
The Sea Venture, sailing ship storm-wrecked	1609	Right off Bermuda
Its rescue boat	1609	Right off Bermuda
Nuestra Senora de Guadalupe's three accompanying galleons	1750	Cape Hatteras off North Carolina coast
Patriot, packet ship carrying Aaron Burr's daughter	1812	In Gulf Stream
Wasp, U. S. warship	1814	Off coast of S. Carolina
The Spray, sloop	1909	
The Cyclops, U. S. N. fuel ship	1918	On way from Barbados to Norfolk, Va.
Porta Noca, passenger ship	1926	Took off from Isle of Pines near Cuba
Sandra, freighter	1957	Out from Savannah
Renovoc, yacht	1958	Took off from Key West
The Enchantress	1965	50 miles southwest of Charleston, S. Carolina
Witchcraft	1967	Off Miami
Scorpion, nuclear powered sub	1968	Off the Azores

Aircraft

Flight 19, 5 avenger bombers	1945	Coming back from Bimini
Martin Mariner, PBM flying boat in search	1945	From Patrick AFB
Star Tiger, commercial airliner	1948	En route from Azores to Bermuda
DC-3 charter flight	1949	
Star Ariel, commercial airliner	1950	En route to Kingston
Air Force Tender	1962	En route Va. to Azores
Private plane	1962	Off Nassau
U. S. Superfortress	since	
British Army Transport	then	
Two U. S. Navy Patrol planes		

John Adams, the country's second elected Chief Executive.

Adams was a stubborn and insistent leader. He could not see the infant United States growing up with anything short of a strong naval force guarding her lifeline of ocean water. The moment he entered the White House, he pushed for a national navy and he pushed hard. Accordingly, the young Congress officially established a Navy of the United States.

It was an act that was inevitable in the mind of any man who had watched the growing problems with the new nation's shipping and commerce routes. Destructive onslaught by pirates of the seas and ferocious attacks by the Barbary powers abroad had fast forced the issue.

Young, handsome and daring Midshipman Johnston Blakeley was glad they had. He now had a career to his liking—a life on the sea, fighting for his adopted country he loved so well.

In May of 1800 when Blakeley entered the Navy, it consisted of about thirty ships in service. He was assigned to a frigate, the *President,* the flagship of Commodore Richard Dale, a 44-gun ship on duty in the trouble-torn Mediteranean. The Commodore was renowned for his Revolutionary experience when he fought valiantly for John Paul Jones on the *Bonhomme Richard.*

It was with this hero of the War of Independence that young Blakeley first tasted battle. He sailed with him into the almost forgotten war with Tripoli.

The following years found the midshipman sailing again and again into the continuing war against the pirates of Tripoli until their ultimate capitulation in 1805. Then he was assigned a tour of duty along the Atlantic coast. By 1807 he was commissioned a lieutenant and saw service at the Norfolk Navy Yard. He was given his first command in March of 1811 and was placed in charge of the *Enterprise*. Only four months later he was commissioned a master commandant.

By the time trouble with Great Britain had exploded into a new war, which Congress declared on June 18, 1812, Johnston Blakeley was an experienced "seadog." In a little over a year, he was given command of one of America's warships—the *Wasp*. His assignment—to seek out ships of the British Merchant Marine and rout them.

No American ship was in better hands. Blakeley was an expert at handling men and there were none better trained or smoother operating than the crews of Captain Blakeley. That was known far and wide.

At the time of the outbreak of hostilities, Great Britain had 800 good fighting ships; the United States' fleet numbered no more than 17 cruisers classified as effective. Still, the young Navy felt redoubtable. With leaders like Blakeley, it had a right to.

The *Wasp* was the second ship bearing that name. The first vessel had become renowned for its bravery after its devastating attack on a British warship in the fall of 1812. It had subsequently been captured. But the replacement was destined to make an even greater fame when it set forth on May 1, 1814 under the hell-bent-for-victory leadership of Captain Johnston Blakeley.

The new *Wasp* was a 22-gun vessel with a

crew of 173 officers and men, most of whom were veterans of wars with the British, Spanish, French and Malayan pirates. Each man knew his job well and had the strong metal with which to perform it.

None more so than the commander.

Blakeley set his course for the crowded waters of the European coast. His goal was to track down and capture the enemy's commerce.

A challenge most meet for just about the newest, handiest and swiftest vessel on the sea.

At four o'clock in the morning of June 28, 1814, the *Wasp* made its first major encounter. A strange ship loomed on the horizon. The weather being cloudy with a light breeze from the northeast, the *Wasp* raised two sails to the windward. The American ship was a well-outfitted vessel carrying 22 guns with about 309 pounds to the broadside. Now everything stood ready.

In a few minutes three other ships appeared close at hand off the weather beam. Blakeley shifted his course for the nearest vessel and by 12:30 p.m. cleared for action.

It proved to be no ship of commerce, but a British brig-of-war. She bore the name, the *Reindeer*.

The brig accepted the bold challenge immediately and hoisted sail to close. She crept steadily up on the weather quarter of the American and at 3:15 p.m. opened fire from a shifting 12-pound carronade upon her forecastle, which was loaded with grape.

Blakeley's ship took five firings of the British gun before it could get itself helm-a-lee and able to fire its carronades from forward direction as it bore.

For the next ten minutes the two ships, heaving side by side no farther apart from each other than the distance of an average city street, kept up a ceaseless exchange of fire. The concussions of the explosions so deadened the wind, that the ships lost way and rolled near blind in an enveloping cloud of smoke.

Both crews worked at the guns with unremitting will and fervor.

Finally, the British commander, Captain William Manners, one of the most renowned officers in the British Navy, reached the conclusion that his only hope in victory lay in that last resource of the warship: the cut of the single cutlass and the individual strong right arm.

By now, the ships were almost touching.

Manners took several shots as he stood at his post, directing the attack. He let the blood pour down one shoulder and his arm as he shouted his commands.

With one sudden movement, at the British captain's order, the *Reindeer* put its helm up and ran the *Wasp* aboard on her port quarter.

At the same moment an American grape shot rammed through the British captain's thighs, dropping him to the deck. He dragged himself again to his feet and clinging to a stay to remain upright, he shouted orders to his men.

"Prepare to board!"

The *Reindeer's* men sprang to the rail, poised for boarding.

Blakeley was ready for them.

The moment the two ships had caught together, he had called his men aft and amassed them behind the rail.

Now in a cloud of thick smoke that blinded the most eager eyes, the two sets of seamen hacked and parried through the ports in the enveloping smoke.

Gradually, in the aftermath of silence from the big guns, the shroud of gunsmoke cleared.

It could be seen now that only a small chasm separated the two vessels. Both sets of seamen thrust at each other in wild hand-to-hand conflict. The top-men and marines on each ship let go with withering fire.

Slowly the English pulled back.

With that, the dying Captain Manners in a burst of gathered strength, his wounds pouring forth blood, sprang to the breach, sword in hand, and leaped to the rail.

"Follow me, men!" he cried.

At that instant, a bullet from the American maintop smashed into his skull. He clasped his left hand to his face and shrieked,

"My God!" Then, with his sword still brandishing in his right hand, he fell to the deck he had fought so hard to defend.

The British sailors hesitated. Their leader was gone. Hope went with him.

In those same seconds, Johnston Blakeley quickly sprang to the rail of the *Reindeer* and shouted,

"Aboard!"

In almost a single wave of forward motion, the American sailors followed their captain over the rail and onto the deck of the English brig, filling the air with wild cheers.

A furious struggle scraped and tore over the British deck. The English were either killed, wounded, or driven below. In minutes, the captain's clerk, the highest surviving officer, surrendered the ship.

The total time of the engagement had been

27 minutes. The results: the *Reindeer* had lost 67 killed and wounded and was herself cut to pieces. The *Wasp,* though severely handled, was holding up well. Her loss had been only 26 killed and wounded.

History recorded the sea battle as the "best fight of them all." There had been no mistakes on either side. It was said later that in no way could Blakeley have ended the fight more quickly than he did. He found the captured vessel too far gone to save. The morning following the battle, after the crew had been removed, the American captain ordered the stricken vessel burned.

After this decisive engagement which raised Johnston Blakeley to international renown, he took his ship into l'Orient, France, to refit. He remained there until August 27th. On that day, he once again hoisted her sails to the winds.

It was September 1st, when the hard-fighting captain pushed into action again. He overhauled a convoy bound for Gibraltar under the protection of a line-of-battle ship, the *Armada 74.*

In spite of the fact he was chased away several times by the line-of-battle ship, he persisted in nettling and darting his way in, until he finally succeeded in cutting out one of the convoy. He overpowered her, boarding and burning the cargo of valuable guns and military equipment right under the nose of its helpless and outraged captain.

All this accomplished without the least harm to his men or his ship!

By half past six that evening, the bold American had run the convoy out of sight and was sailing the sea with all eyes alert.

Suddenly the lookout aloft spied four vessels

in the evening light—two to starboard; two to port. Captain Blakeley gave orders to approach them. He wished a nearer look at them. It was a wonder to his men that not a thought of concern seemed to enter the captain's mind that they might all be ships-of-war they be heading for. It would have made no difference to him if they were, they knew.

Blakeley found an interesting bag of contents! The rows of sails proved to be three English war vessels chasing a fourth ship—an American privateer!

At seven o'clock, the nearest British ship, which turned out to be the formidable brig-of-war, the *Avon* captained by John Arbuthnot and carrying 20 guns, lagged intentionally behind the others.

Through the darkness around eight o'clock, the *Avon* put out night signals.

Blakeley paid no attention. At 8:38 p.m. the British ship began firing her stern chaser. But within the hour, despite this action, the *Wasp* had succeeded in weathering on the *Avon* off the port quarter. Hails were exchanged. The brig was ordered to heave to. She declined to and set her foretopmast studding sail to escape.

The *Wasp* let go with a 12-pound carronade. The *Avon's* stern guns replied. Blakeley then, fearing that the English would square away before the wind and elude him in the darkness, shifted his helm and ran to leeward of her. Ranging alongside, he poured a raking broadside into her starboard quarter as he passed. A wild outbreak of fighting ensued. The night was intensely black and all the seamen of the *Wasp* could pick out in the darkness gliding beside them was one long shadow darting along on the waves.

All they could aim their fire at were the flashes of the enemy's guns or at the white foam on her water-line. As usual, their aim was skillful and the results effective.

Before long the *Avon's* guns were dismounted and the mainmast carried away. After a half hour, she was completely silenced. Blakeley suspended his fire and asked if the *Avon* had struck. She finally answered that she had.

The *Avon's* crew suffered losses of 42 killed and wounded; the *Wasp's* loss was two killed and one wounded. The British ship went down, bow foremost. The American vessel slipped off into the night. She could see she was being approached by three other English ships of war. Being vastly outnumbered and overpowered, the *Wasp* turned tail and ran. The British vessels failed to pursue, for they turned their attention to the sinking *Avon.*

The American hero and his daredevil crew continued on their course. All through the following weeks and months, the cocky little warship created havoc among English merchant vessels and privateers. She had so stung the enemy and racked up such a record in the young American Navy, that she became the envy of the entire battle fleet. The very name, *Wasp,* had come to stand for hard fighting, bravery and above all—success.

In October, the stout-beamed ship captured a prize: the *Atlanta,* an English merchantman so valuable, Blakeley sent her back to the States with a prize crew. She docked at Savannah, Georgia, on November 4th. She carried Blakeley's personal report of all his engagements to the Secretary of the Navy.

That was the last word ever received from Johnston Blakeley.

A few weeks later, a Swedish brig, the *Adonis*, reported an incident. While carrying two American lieutenants from a captured British ship, she ran across the American ship. The *Adonis* requested to board the two officers onto the *Wasp*. The men gratefully changed ships and the Wasp sailed serenely on. Her next stop, it's always been believed, was intended to be a port in South Carolina.

From that moment to this, there has never been heard one more word about the fighting, courageous American ship. She pulled away from the *Adonis* with salutes and cries of farewell. Be that as it may, she made for the horizon, her canvas bellying to the wind on that long ago day in October. She was headed in a southwest direction—right for the mid-Atlantic Danger Zone!

As an added strange note, it is interesting to note that the first *Wasp*, which had been captured by the British in 1812 and taken into their service, sailed away on a cruise in that same year of 1814. Like her younger namesake, she never came back. She was never hard from again.

Both ships disappeared in the distant mists of the sea as readily as if they had sailed into some far-away ocean Valhalla!

There are still some sailors in the world who declare that they did.

Chapter Five

What happened during the last few hours aboard the ENCHANTRESS will always be a mystery, forever locked in the sea . . .

Statement by Frank Davis, first skipper of the *Enchantress* on her last voyage.

THEY SAILED INTO OBLIVION

The unexplained disappearance of Blakeley and his *Wasp* may have been the first recorded U.S. Navy vessel-vanishing, but certainly not its last.

That branch of the United States military services has seen several subsequent tragedies just as mysterious. Instances such as the famous case of the fuel ship, the *Cyclops*, U.S.N. That large 14,500 ton supply ship vanished sometime after March 4th, 1918 on her way from Barbados to Norfolk, Virginia, bearing a cargo of much-needed manganese ore for the Allies in World War 1.

The theory that she had been sunk by German submarines was the first thought advanced but that proved to be unfounded when after the war it was determined that no enemy subs were in the area at that time. Like her predecessors the *Cyclops* simply sank into a far Unknown leaving not a crumb of debris, lifeboats or bodies. A huge vessel with over 300 people vanished utterly. No conclusions as to her fate were forthcoming from an Inquiry Board in 1918. An answer may be supplied shortly, however, for, as of this writing, word has come out that the wreckage of the famed *Cyclops* has finally been located. More detailed information will be eagerly awaited by Bermuda Triangle fans.

But it was not just the U.S. Navy that came to suffer loss in the Mid-Atlantic Danger Zone. Commercial vessels as well as private yachts over the years have been sweeping over some strange invisible salt-water barrier into the sea-green Mystery Zone.

In 1950 the *Sandra*, a 350-foot freighter sailed from Miami for Savannah. There 300 tons of insecticide were loaded on board destined for Puerto Cabello, Venezuela. Pulling out from that Georgia port, the *Sandra* chunked confidently towards South America. She furrowed the Atlantic waters into rippling channels as she cleared port. It was the last sight of her ever caught by man. What could have happened to her and the 28 men aboard? No one has the least idea. Not a trace of her was ever found. Nor was the *Sandra* the last freighter to vanish in the coastal waters.

Last March 21st of 1973, the huge 13,000 ton German freighter, *Anita*, laden with a cargo of coal, steamed out of Newport News, Virginia, headed for Germany. She never made it. The *Anita*, like so many before her, was swept into oblivion with her crew of 32 men.

Lloyd's of London recently penned the freighter's name at the bottom of its long list of "missing" ships, making the total of 60 vessels and 937 persons over the past ten years.

A small commercial venture once met with disaster in the waters off Cuba. A Caribbean passenger ship, the *Porta Noca*, operated a service from Tampa, Florida, to the Isles of Pines and Grand Cayman Isle off the coast of Cuba, returning to Tampa.

Residents on the tiny Cuban isles relied on the *Porta Noca* to get them from place to place in the early years of this century.

One of those people was the late Rad Miller.

What occurred to him while living on the Isle of Pinés in 1926 was a story Miller knew well. He told it from time to time with a thoughtful faraway look in his eyes. Although Rad Miller didn't know it at the time, he came very close to being a visitor to the depths of the Bermuda Triangle!

An artist who spent much of his life in the environs of New Hope, Pennsylvania, and the very last years in Raven Rock, New Jersey, Miller loved to recall the fruitful year of his youth when he lived on the Isle of Pines.

It was an island of primitive beauty at that time though it was fast becoming the faraway hideout spa for wealthy Cubans. In later years after Castro's coming to power, the place was turned into a new use—a penal isle.

But in 1926 for Rad Miller it was a painter's paradise. The unspoiled beauty of soft sand sprouting reaches of scrub pines gave him untold inner peace and inspiration with which to create.

For a change, he occasionally took a boat to some of the surrounding islands to paint.

On a fresh-aired morning in the summer of '26, Rad packed up his paints, brushes, canvases, and a change of clothes and started out for the island dock. He had just enough time to catch the *Porta Noca*. He would "island hop" and get off where he felt like it.

As he wound down the sandy path towards

the Gerona dock, he could see the white form of the *Porta Noca* tugging gently at her ropes. He started to whistle as he hurried his long legs along the sun-lit path, his painting equipment tucked under one arm and his small overnight case in the other hand. It was such a flawless day . . .

Rad raised his eyes as he started down the last stretch of roadway. Suddenly he stopped cold right where he was. The ship ahead of him no longer looked a welcome glistening white. She was bathed in a diffused glow as though she were shimmering with lights hidden by mist. The entire scene of the natives bending at their tasks and the little string of passengers leaning on the rail seemed veiled. The whole view looked like a Turner painting of a sea's edge shrouded in fog.

In the next instant the vision disappeared. The ship rocked normally once more at its moorings, bright in the island sunlight.

Rad slowed up his pace as he approached the dock. One of the passengers pushed back a yellowed Panama hat from his forehead and studied intently the ship's hands as they labored on the wharf beneath him. The captain leaned out of the pilot house, stared for a moment at the artist, then shouted out an order to a seaman on the deck.

There was little time left, Rad knew. One more minute and the ship would pull out without him.

Still he felt rooted to the spot where he stood. Something kept him from his usual confident pace and the signal of greeting he customarily gave forth.

He stayed where he was, dropping his baggage at his feet. With a hand that felt numb, he shielded his eyes against the glare and watched the *Porta Noca* slip free of the dock and ease out to sea.

Slowly, the artist walked back to his cottage. What kind of idiot was he? To let just a feeling, like a wall, well up inside him and keep him from a trip he'd so made up his mind to? Literally bind him from moving?

For the rest of his life, Rad Miller blessed that instinct. It saved his life. The *Porta Noca* after leaving Gerona dock was never caught sight of again. She never landed at any other island port. In weather that was without a sliver of cloud and in a sea that was calm as bath water! Nothing could be conceived of that might have caused trouble to the little ship. She seemed to glide out into a perfect afternoon and leave the face of the globe!

Rad followd the mystery closely but not a single sensible solution ever came forth from the various investigations that searched diligently for a clue. There wasn't a remnant of life preserver nor a piece of clothing and, completely unexplainable since the *Porta Noca* was a diesel-operated ship, not a sign of oil slick floating on the water. Such a thing seemed a near impossibility. Yet it was the case.

Such is the story of one of the smaller but most intriguing mysteries in that baffling area.

Not only commercial vessels, however, have met their doom in those puzzling waters. Privately-owned yachts have carried their owners, frequently with family or guests, to the same nether-regions of a bizarre destiny.

Many of these individuals were well-known

people of their day . . . but none of more historic importance than Joshua Slocum.

Captain Slocum is known in the annals of sailing history as "America's best known sailor." One couldn't think of a better or more deserved reputation for the first man to sail alone around the world.

Joshua Slocum performed this fantastic feat in 1897 . . . a 46,000 mile adventure that earned him a place in history.

Slocum was a native Nova Scotian. He was born on Brier's Island . . . a birthplace heritage that was to serve him well. Not only were the islanders there superb fishermen, they were their own shipbuilders. Joshua was no exception to this talent. He spent his youth accumulating every aspect of that national inheritance, learning to fish with the best and build with the greatest know-how in the world.

As soon as he'd reached adult years, he was off to use his skills. He burrowed a deep and colorful swath of adventure in seas all over the globe. He commanded a successful voyage to northern Alaskan waters and later captained a San Francisco-to-Honolulu packet. In subsequent years, he sailed to the Philippine Islands, setting up a brisk trading business with the natives. Later he got involved in trade with China. By the late 1800's there wasn't a better known name from continent to continent than Captain Joshua Slocum.

But this wasn't enough. Joshua Slocum had a dream. He'd had it since he was sixteen. He wanted to sail a ship around the world—alone!

Few men took him seriously, save those who knew his guts and grit. Too foolhardy to consider, said the seamen of his day. But Joshua was all hardiness and little folly. He ceased all voyages for a time and returned to Nova Scotia to build himself an earth-girdling vessel that was the sea-worthiest ship of all time. When he was finished he named his 36-foot sloop, the *Spray*.

On a cool day in 1897, the indomitable Slocum unfurled his sails to the North Atlantic winds and set forth. Welcomed from port to port all over the world, the courageous captain completed his 46,000 mile trek before the year was out. He had accomplished his youthful dream.

His success shot him to instant fame all over the globe. His name was not only a byword at every port; it was the social center of conversation in every salon and palace of every nation. He was deluged by newspapers and publishers for accounts of his experiences. He was assailed by promoters and bureaus to lecture for audiences in clubs and societies. So Captain Slocum came to spend more time with memoirs and club members than with his *Spray*. He didn't like it.

He withdrew from the public and retired to the village of West Tisbury on Martha's Vineyard, his only neighbors just other old sea captains like himself.

With a wit as salty as the seas he loved so well, he always gave a terse and meaningful answer to his questioners. When asked why he had chosen to retire to West Tisbury, of all the places he'd seen in the world, he said with a sniff of the nostrils and a twinkle of the eye, that it was because of the dates on the tombstones there, for by them he "concluded that this was about as healthy a place as (he) could find!"

But Joshua Slocum was not destined to lie beneath that West Tisbury sod. He was to join the lost seamen of the past in a mysterious area he had never thought of as a puzzle, only a pleasure—the Caribbean.

For the years of 1905, '07 and '08, Slocum spent glorious winters far from the black-tie banquets that had come to bore him so much. He sailed on his beloved *Spray*—alone, of course —to Grand Cayman Island not far from Jamaica. He loved the old buccaneer hide-out. The speech of the soft-tongued islanders with its quaint and archaic patois was a sure outgrowth of the old pirate lingo. It carried for him the flavor of the great seadogs' talk of the past. Men like Sir Francis Drake and Henry Morgan came to life for him on Grand Cayman.

But life for Slocum was nearing an end as adventurous as its beginnings.

In the year 1909 Captain Slocum outfitted the *Spray* for his Caribbean voyage at the Herreshoff works at Bristol, Rhode Island. "Nat" Herreshoff himself inspected the craft and pronounced it in top shape.

With a goodly wind at his heels, Slocum guided his *Spray* out of Bristol harbor. Well outfitted and provided for, the experienced ship headed southwards. Joshua himself stood at the wheel with weather-brown face alight with clear-staring eyes. He'd never been in better health, declared his son later who had visited with him shortly before the fatal voyage.

Like so many sailors before him, Joshua Slocum cleared port, glided out into a calm sea and sailed away into oblivion. He was never seen again. Nor any spar or slip of canvas from the *Spray*. The two partners of old disappeared from human sight.

In trying to fit the pieces of the puzzle together, Joshua's son, Victor, could find little to go on. There was good weather all along the coast at that time. If fire had broken out, the ship was well equipped to handle the emergency. And even, failing in this, there would be some vestige of floating wood to tell the tale. An explosion seemed so unlikely as to be impossible and even then, remnants of splintered wood would be found floating.

But there was nothing ever found. Not a sign of the renowned captain or his famous vessel was ever picked up.

Victor Slocum found only one possible solution. His father's ship had been run down in the night by a transoceanic liner.

This explanation was difficult to accept for those at Gloucester, Massachusetts, who had known the captain well and had entertained him on many occasions. As a farewell gift for the hardy adventurer, the men of Gloucester had presented Slocum with a very special gift . . . a light for the *Spray* which highlighted the sails like a beacon to avoid any danger of nighttime collision.

Joshua had coughed a bemused throat-clearing when he accepted the present and commented with a wry smile that there could be as much possibility of a ship running him down in the dark now as for a vessel to ram a lightship!

How could any liner have failed to spot the *Spray*, her sails aglow like a beacon in the dark with the Gloucester light?

As always, no answer to the puzzle has ever been a satisfactory one. Captain Joshua Slocum became one more name in the roll call of the Mystery Zone's "captured" seamen.

Recent times has sent a modern captain to meet with Joshua—millionaire yachtsman, Harvey Conover.

Conover dubbed his yacht an unusual nomen —his name spelled backwards: *Revonoc*. Both the giver and the recipient went down to an unknown fate in January of 1958.

Conover was not only a highly successful businessman, president of the Conover-Nast Publications, Inc. of New York which put out *Aviation Age* and other technical magazines, but an experienced flyer (he'd been a World War I pilot in the Air Corps) and a renowned yachtsman. The millionaire sailor had won the Miami-to-Nassau race on three occasions . . . and with good reason, said his colleagues. His yawl was the supreme in construction. It was called the "safest and finest craft afloat."

And it was—until New Year's Day of 1958 when *Revonoc* sailed south into the Bermuda Triangle! It was her last adventure.

It was a Wednesday. The day dawned fair with no suggestion of any weather problems. The *Revonoc* party assembled at the dock at Key West, Florida. There were Captain Conover's wife, Dorothy, and their 27 year old son, Lawrence. Also accompanying the Conover family for the voyage was a couple who were good friends of the publisher and his family, the William Fluegelmans of Scarsdale, New York.

Mrs. Fluegelman grew squeamish about the trip. The prospect of being trapped at sea on a heaving yacht suddenly began to panic her. As much fun as the trip promised to be, she decided to withdraw from it at the last minute.

William Fluegelman kissed his wife goodbye and leaped aboard.

They never saw each other again.

The *Revonoc* swept outwards towards the sea with her sails white and full against the harbor's blue waters. Captain Conover exchanged greetings with the other craft dotting the bay as his slim yawl sped past one ship after another.

By Saturday, after not a sign of the dazzling yacht had been spotted at any Caribbean port, a friend of Harvey Conover's called the Miami Coast Guard. He was concerned. So was the Coast Guard. A storm had struck the area a few days before and the Gulf Stream had been rocked by heavy waves at that time.

The Coast Guard launched one of the most intense air and sea searches Florida had ever known. Every port on every island in the area was checked, as well. Not a sign of the *Revonoc* had been seen by anyone, anywhere.

Planes scanned the region from Delray Beach to Fort Pierce and eastward past the Bahamas. Even the Cuban Navy joined the search. In all, over 100,000 square miles of ocean was combed. Only one thing was found: on January 6th, the *Revonoc's* 12-foot dinghy, *Revonoc, Jr.*, was located on a beach about 80 miles north of Miami. It appeared she had been pulled from her mountings.

All of which told nothing about what happened to the "safest craft afloat" and her crew, all of whom were experienced sailors. The 44-foot yawl with all four people aboard had vanished without leaving a trace. It seemed impossible. The staunch yacht and her capable crew could have easily endured the Gulf Stream storm. She had on many a former occasion. And even if she had gone under, why would there not be floating debris or remains of her passengers swept ashore on the beach as was her dinghy?

How could every sign of ship and passengers simply disappear in an area heavily trafficked by ships without some hint of what happened or of something being seen somewhere by someone?

It could and did happen to the Harvey Conover family and their friend, as it has occurred for years to hundreds of other travelers throughout the Bermuda Triangle.

Almost six years later, when the *Revonoc* tragedy had dimmed in the memory of man, the stage was set for a new drama in the Triangle. *Motor Boating* magazine carried a communication in its Letters-to-the-Editor department from a man well-known in yachting circles. He was Count Christopher de Grabowski.

Renowned for his daring as an adventurer and a sailor, the count had once crossed the Atlantic alone from Tangier to New York City in his 25-foot cutter, *Tethys*.

In that clear spring of '64 a new adventure awaited the Polish outdoorsman. He was so enthusiastic over it, he wrote about it in the reader's column of *Motor Boating*.

Dear Editor:

. . . I hope to sail on January 7 or 8 directly for St. Thomas. . . . I shall be skippering *Enchantress,* a pretty fifty-nine foot schooner on an extensive voyage—six months and 8,000 miles. Her owner, who will bring his wife

The first Bermuda landmark sighted from the sea or air is the Gibbs Hill Light, one of the brightest navigational beacons in the world. How many tragic disappearances has it shone over?

UPI

Christopher Columbus was the first known voyager to the Bermuda Triangle. He and his men saw "a remarkable ball of fire" fall into the sea and were terrified by a baffling disturbance of the ship's compass.

Once Vice-President of the United States, once tried for treason, once an exile... Aaron Burr in 1812 was a lonely man. His one comfort was his beautiful and intelligent daughter Theodosia, wife of Joseph Alston, Governor of South Carolina. On December 31 she boarded the packet ship *Patriot* to travel from Georgetown harbor to New York City to see her father.

The weather was fair and the wind moderate. In minutes the little ship was gliding swiftly out to sea. It was never seen again. Was Theodosia's ship attacked by pirates? War-time sabotage? No one knows for sure. The disappearance of the *Patriot* ranks high in any list of unexplained vanishings in the Atlantic's danger zone.

Trouble with Great Britain had exploded into the War of 1812 and young Johnston Blakely was given command of the *Wasp*, one of America's warships. He won great victories against the *Reindeer*, the *Avon*, the *Atlanta* and other British ships. Then, in October, 1814, he made his last contact with civilization and headed southwest...to the Bermuda Triangle!

On March 21, 1973, the huge 13,000 ton German freighter, *Anita*, laden with a cargo of coal, steamed out of Newport News, Virginia, headed for Germany. She never made it. The *Anita*, like so many before her, was swept into oblivion with her crew of 32 men. Lloyd's of London recently penned the freighter's name at the bottom of its long list of "missing" ships, making the total of 60 vessels and 937 persons over the past ten years.

Joshua Slocum, "America's best known sailor," was the first man to sail alone around the world. He performed this fantastic feat in 1897...a 46,000 mile adventure in his 36-foot sloop, the *Spray*. In 1909, he left on a Caribbean cruise and was never seen again. No trace of the *Spray* was ever found.

Long a part of sailors' lore, eerie and manless Ghost Ships have been a heart-chilling sight in the Devil's Triangle,

What happened to the *Scorpion*? Last heard from on May 21, 1968, this SKIPJACK-class nuclear powered submarine went down mysteriously 500 miles southwest of the Azores. **Below:** Harvey Conover was a successful businessman and re-knowned yachtsman. On New Year's Day, 1958, he sailed with his family into the Bermuda Triangle. The "safest craft afloat" disappeared without a trace!

A TBM *Avenger* Torpedo Bomber. Five of these aircraft made up the famous *lost patrol* of 1945.

UPI

Top: The Office of Naval Research made a study of the possibility of gravitational disturbance. **Top Left:** A frightening incident—total instrument failure—over the Devil's Sea changed Arthur Godfrey's mind about the existence of "danger zones." **Bottom Left:** The late scientist Ivan Sanderson came to believe that there were civilizations of superior intelligence under the sea. **Below:** Einstein theorized that *time* is the fourth dimension. Is time the key to the Bermuda Triangle mystery?

Bettmann Archive

**Linking past and present,
the mystery of the Bermuda Triangle continues.**

along, is a southern California insurance man completely new to yachting.

We sail from Charleston to California via the Windward Islands and Panama. I'm looking forward to this trip. . .

Chris de Grabowski
Charleston, S. C.

The insurance man Grabowski spoke of was, indeed, a man new to the sport of yachting. He was John L. Pelton of Whittier, California. On November 17th of 1963 the would-be voyager had come to New York City and purchased his first yacht. It was called, the *Enchantress*.

The craft was not new but she was in good condition. She had been built at the Bath Iron Works, Maine, in 1925. Her overall length was 59 feet; her tonnage 20. Her decks were all of teak and her trim was of mahogany and teak. Her sails were in good condition. She also carried the auxiliary power of a Gray marine engine. Recently she'd had a radio direction finder and a radio ship-to-shore telephone installed. She was also well equipped with life jackets, life belts and an eight-foot fiberglass lifeboat.

Mr. Pelton was delighted. This purchase and his proposed voyage were a life's dream come true.

The new owner, although he'd had some experience in small power boats, had no knowledge of sail craft. He was now eager to learn. He searched diligently for a skipper. He found him in the person of the manager of a Massachusetts boatyard, Captain Frank Davis.

But Captain Davis didn't want to be on duty over Christmas. So, with the understanding he could leave the *Enchantress* on time to join his family for the holiday he agreed to set sail with Pelton on November 28th of 1964.

The *Enchantress* had a windy day heading along the coast. Southeast winds hit her with gusts from 35 to 50 knots. She weathered the assault without a problem, arriving in Charleston harbor on December 13th.

It was at this port that a new captain was signed up for the balance of the voyage. Pelton latched on to a yachtsman extremely experienced and well-known. He was Count Christopher de Grabowski.

The count had a record of over 50,000 miles of sailing between 1958 and '63 alone. He also bore the honor of being the vice-commodore of the "Slocum Society," that organization formed many years ago in honor of Joshua Slocum.

Little did Grabowski dream as he guided the yacht out of Charlestown harbor on January 10, 1964 that he, too, like Joshua, so many years before him, was heading for his greatest and most inexplicable adventure—a voyage into the Bermuda Triangle—the trip of no-return. With him would be the boat's owner and his wife and two small sons.

The shining craft flew like a blue gull along the Carolina shore, her white wings wide, headed for St. Thomas in the Virgin Islands.

Her glory was to be brief. Three days later, the Coast Guard Station at Jacksonville Beach Station heard a distress call come in. It was from the *Enchantress*. She was in trouble having run into a gale off Florida.

The Coastguardsman requested the *Enchantress* to start a long count so that their exact position could be ascertained.

A man's voice started the count. A few minutes later a child's voice took it up, counting on and on, until the tones got weaker and weaker. Soon the voice faded out completely.

The craft's position was estimated at 150 miles southeast of Charleston. The Coast Guard's Search and Rescue Squad was on the run in minutes. Navy vessels joined the hunt which ultimately covered an area of over 12,000 square miles.

Although the rescue units were hurried to the spot, not a sign of the craft was seen.

Not a vestige of anything that could be related to the *Enchantress* could be found. As always, no pieces of rail or sail or human bodies. Nothing.

The old, old story had been enacted once again in the mysterious waters of the Bermuda Triangle.

Only three years later, in December of 1967, the same drama filled the stage of the southern waters, cuing actors very much like the yachtsmen of earlier years. This time the roles were filled by two Floridians. One was the owner of a Miami Beach hotel, Dan Burrack, and the other was a close friend and churchman, Father Patrick Horgan of St. George's Catholic Church in Fort Lauderdale.

Burrack's yacht *Witchcraft* was a 23-foot boat that carried as much confidence as any craft could. She was considered unsinkable because of her type of construction. She had real stay-afloat insurance: built-in flotation chambers guaranteed to keep her sink-proof.

She also carried aboard ample supply of floating cushions and life-jackets.

If there was one thing Burrack wasn't worried

about, it was ever going down in his unsinkable jolly *Witchcraft!*

It wasn't even a suggestion on his mind on that fateful December night when he and Father Horgan decided to take the little craft on a cruise about a mile offshore to see Miami's brilliant skyline after dark. The town looked like a Christmas tree dazzling with flickering lights and silver tinsel.

A little after 9 p.m. the Coast Guard received a radio message from the hotel owner that the *Witchcraft* had struck some underwater object. However, Burrack stressed, the blow was a glancing one that merely bent the propellers and had not damaged the craft itself. They were taking in no water. His problem was minor but required, nevertheless, assistance. The bent propellors were causing vibrations that prevented the boat from operating properly. Could he have a tow back to harbor?

Three minutes later, a Coast Guard crew was in the water cutting quickly towards the *Witchcraft's* position.

Within 15 minutes, the Coast Guard cutter arrived at the given location. There wasn't a sign of the cabin cruiser. Nothing but a channel buoy bobbing in the starlight.

The Coast Guard tried to raise a response on the radio from the yacht, but they were answered only by silence.

A search was instituted that reached from Key West to Jacksonville and over 200 miles out to sea. But not a trace could be found of either Burrack, Father Horgan, the cruiser itself or of any of its equipment or flotation gear. They all vanished without a clue as to what happened.

Once more the curtains dropped down on a drama at sea that had no ending.

As they have been doing all through the years from time to time, sturdy freighters and white-winged yachts have voyaged along with merchantmen of old and battleships of every era into some great Unknown . . . the puzzle of our era. A mysterious drama, not just in the colorful creativity of man's mind, but baffling disappearances officially substantiated by Navy and Coast Guard records.

A puzzling plot that seems to be ever thickening.

Chapter Six

We might just as well have searched a painted ship on a painted ocean for sight of the vanished crew.

Statement by a federal government official at the end of the investigation into the mystery of the *Carroll A. Deering*.

GHOST SHIPS
OF THE TRIANGLE

One of the stranger aspects of the Bermuda Triangle mystery over the years is the occasional discovery of a manless vessel in its waters.

There is an eeriness to a "dead ship" that is more flesh-creeping and more awesome than a complete obliteration of everything. Coming face-to-face with a "ghost ship" is heart-chilling fare.

Ask anyone who has had the experience.

Like the crew of the S.S. *Aztec* that came boiling into port at Bristol, England, in 1935 and reported a ghost ship was riding the waves off Bermuda. Every man on board had seen it. It was no figment of imagination.

Talk rattled about the Bristol wharves for days. Long a nerve-center for shipping tendrons leading to North America since the earliest days (John Cabot sailed from there for North America in 1497, returning grandly with claims for the crown), she had always been a good rumor spa for ghost ship sightings.

But all that was different. This was no phantom, declared the seamen aboard the S.S. *Aztec*. She was a solid matter ship with the name *La Dahama* painted on her hull. In fact, several of the crew members had boarded the stricken vessel and retrieved her abandoned log-book, as untouched and unmarred by disaster as though the captain had just put his pen down and walked away!

It had been a shocker to come upon the lifeless ship, said the *Aztec* men, her beams swaying this way and that with the currents crossing and recrossing the Bermuda seas. Something terrible had obviously struck out at what had once been a beautiful sailing yacht. Her skylights were smashed; her rudder was broken and her masts were trailing overboard.

There wasn't a sign of a survivor from whatever disaster had hit it.

Old seamen in Bristol puffed on their pipes and nodded thoughtfully. Memories were reborn of the old tale of the *Mary Celeste* found abandoned in the Atlantic in 1872. No solution was ever found to explain what caused that vessel to be so swiftly and mysteriously abandoned or what became of the crew.

Then something happened that astonished the participants in the *Aztec* experience.

Shortly after the return of that ship, an Italian liner, the *Rex* pulled into port with a veritable adventure story. In the waters off Bermuda some days before, the liner had come upon a stricken ship. Her name was *La Dahama*. The crew was battling hopelessly to save the craft which was sinking rapidly, her masts had snapped and were trailing overboard.

Quickly the *Rex* approached and picked up the captain and seamen from the doomed vessel just in time before the sailing ship was sucked rapidly under.

Rocked by a sudden squall that had hit them,

the crew told of their losing battle to save the
wind and wave-smashed ship.

The crew of the lost ship and of the *Rex* as
well as the men and women passengers aboard
the luxury liner watched in awe as the waves
splurged up over the sinking *Dahama*. With a
heave the vessel with its broken masts slowly
slipped from sight. In just minutes there was
not a sign left of the ship but a few fragments
of spars and sail canvas. She had joined her
sisters of a fatal past in Davy Jones' Locker beneath the sea.

Or had she?

The crew of the *Aztec* denied that this could
have been possible. They had witnessed the *La
Dahama* still very much afloat *after* the *Rex* had
seen her go under! They had the log to prove
they'd been aboard!

Could a ship sink and rise again from the
depths of an ocean to haunt the Atlantic?

Many sailors believe it could. And that in the
Bermuda Triangle zone in 1935 the *La Dahama*
did!

Those who spend their lives on the sea will
tell you they meet with weird experiences. Seamen may not talk about them easily. They may
not ask you to accept what they say. But they
do believe themselves—many of them—that
strange things happen on the wide wastes of
the world's waters that neither science nor
philosophy can explain.

Like the inexplicable incident of an abandoned vessel that happened some years before
the *Dahama* in that same sea-zone of mystery.
The odd puzzle of the *Carroll A. Deering*.

It all had a weird beginning. On a clear, cold
dawn in early February of 1921, the morning

watch at the Cape Hatteras Coast Guard station off North Carolina's Outer Banks spied an awesome spectacle! On the Diamond Shoals a five-masted schooner with full sail catching the wind, was straining vainly against the beach, her prow thrust deep into the sand!

The watchmen at the station were nonplussed. How could the ship have gotten there? And why? There had been no storm the night before. In fact, the previous watch had left a report of all clear and calm; no sign of sail, smoke or lights shown nor distress signals of any kind from sea or shore.

Now, suddenly, heaved a ship against the shoals who had signalled no trouble in the night and who now seemed utterly and eerily silent.

The Hatteras Guard launched a power lifeboat and drew as close to the jammed vessel as it could in a choppy early morning sea. The men read the name of the schooner: the *Carroll A. Deering*. She was obviously recently built and an able ship, with sails of new cloth. But there was not a sign of a soul on board. Not a figure outlined itself against the morning sun on the deck or within the rigging. Not a voice responded to the calls of the lifeboat crew. The Deering's jibs and topsails were still unfurled, indicating to the coastguardsmen that nobody had attempted to move the ship off the grounding shoals.

Continuing to survey the mysterious scene, the Coast Guard noticed that the schooner was bereft of lifeboats. There was also a ladder hanging over her port side. The ship had obviously been abandoned. But why? And when? The vessel seemed in most seaworthy condition. And with the weather as fine as it had been

for several days, there was no reason for her
not to be.

Back at the beach station, the Coast Guard
checked out the ship in the Marine Register.
The owner of the *Carroll A. Deering* was the
G. G. Deering Company of Portland, Maine.
She was a $200,000 schooner of 2,114 tons and
had been built at Bath, Maine the year before—
1920.

Immediately, the Coast Guard notified the
Deering Company and promptly a cutter from
Wilmington, North Carolina, and assisting crews
from several nearby Coast Guard stations hurried to the scene to help.

After a complete and thorough search of
every corner, keg and barrel, the Coast Guard
crews turned up exactly one living creature—
a thin, grey cat, so starved, she was mewing
louder than the shrill February wind.

The entire crew of the vessel had vanished.

Also gone were the ship's papers, charts, and
nautical instruments.

The entire schooner was as intact as though
the crewmen, as systematically on that last day
as on every other, had all done their chores then
quietly left. The ship's gear was all in place.
Her stores and signal flags were stowed without
disturbance. Her bunks were all carefully made
up. And, most mysterious of all, the tables were
set with food on every plate, partially consumed,
as though the men had abruptly risen for some
reason that came without warning. Something
had occurred so swiftly, they had pushed back
their chairs from the tables and left! The remaining supply of cooked food, still awaiting
cries for seconds—lay untouched in partially
filled pots on the stove, now cold. Still burning

in the ship's salon were the lights, as though officers in there had gotten up, fully expecting to return in a short time.

Obviously, they never had. They, too, had upped in extreme haste and departed the ship for some unknown and, perhaps, terrifying cause.

What could that reason have been?

The Coast Guard, in an effort to piece together what had happened to the deserted ship, before long had gathered the following facts:

In August of the previous year, the *Deering* had pulled out of Newport News, Virginia, with a cargo of coal. She had headed for Rio de Janeiro under the command of Captain William Merritt of Portland, Maine. The captain's son was his first mate.

Almost from the start, strange things had occurred; the captain, a few days after the voyage had begun, put in at Lewes, Delaware. He reported that he was sick and asked to be taken to a hospital. He was. His son left the ship equally abruptly and went with him.

Notified of the emergency, the managers in Portland ordered replacements. The new captain was William B. Wormell of Boston who was on assignment in New York. When notified of his new command, Wormell promptly checked out of New York and headed for the waiting *Deering* in Lewes. With him, he took an experienced and trustworthy first mate.

Wormell had spent a near-lifetime on the oceans of the world. He'd fought typhoons in the China Sea and had faced the fury of hurricanes in the North Atlantic. There wasn't a brig or schooner under sail he couldn't handle with ease.

What was even more important, he had the reputation of being able to handle a crew. They respected and admired him. He was hardy and likeable as New England stew.

The *Deering* crew of Danes, Finns and one Negro hailed the new commander with good will and put to with a vim to get the long-delayed voyage under way. It was by now early September and the schooner was once more headed for Rio.

After unloading her cargo of coal at the South American port, the captain awaited orders. Learning there was to be no returning cargo, Wormell pulled his schooner out of Rio, clearing the port "light" on December 3rd.

Her next stop was at Barbados. There Wormell learned orders awaited him to sail "light" for Norfolk, Virginia. But in port there in the West Indies, the old-time seafaring captain did an unusual thing: he complained to his company's agents at Bridgetown in Barbados of not feeling well.

But the ill health did not seem to be major enough to warrant his leaving the ship and once again, on January 9, 1921, the *Deering* was putting to sea, leaving the Barbados behind her.

It was the last time she was ever to clear port.

By the afternoon of January 23rd, the schooner was sailing easily by the Cape Fear lightship off the coast of North Carolina. She was clearly spotted by the Coast Guard watch at that point.

But it was six days later that she was again sighted leaning in the wind as she curved past the Cape Lookout lightship off the Diamond Shoals. The distance she had covered from one lightship to the other was only eighty miles! And she'd taken nearly a week to sail it!

Where had she been and what had she been doing for that undue length of time in those off-coast waters?

As with many a mysterious voyage in that Mystery Zone, subsequent investigators of the puzzle would not be able to unravel a single clue that could tell the tale.

The only story they were to uncover was an incident related by the captain of the Cape Lookout Lightship. He stated that when the *Deering* passed him on January 29th, a man was standing on the deck who hailed him through a megaphone. He called that the ship had lost her anchors in a storm. He requested that other ships be on the watch for her as she approached Norfolk.

The captain replied his acceptance of the message but there was an odd feeling he declared as he did so. The man on the schooner's deck, somehow, did not appear to be the ship's captain. He neither looked like a commanding officer nor acted like one. And the crew, he discerned with concern, did not appear to be performing like a proper functioning crew. They were scattered about the vessel in such a way as to indicate lack of conformity or discipline.

The thought of something strange having occurred on board that ship, flashed through the head of the Lightship captain—then was gone. Why should there be anything unusual? He dismissed the slight apprehension and went on with his duties.

But his later testimony concerning this incident was not lightly taken. It was the only significant telltale sign the Board of Inquiry had.

Examining the Lightship captain's description minutely, it was found the *Deering* man on the deck did not tally with the physical appearance of Captain Wormell.

Where, then, had the captain been? What had happened to him? What had delayed the vessel so many days? No storm, however severe, could have caused such a long lapse of time sailing between the two lightships. Nor was there any report of a storm in those waters at that time.

One of the most intensive searches in maritime history followed those perplexing questions. Before it was through, six government agencies besides the Coast Guard became involved: the Navy, Treasury, State, Navigation and Commerce Departments as well as the Justice. The latter came into the case when the possibility of foul play became a possibility. The chance that pirates, even in that era of modern commerce, had attacked and taken over the ship.

Such a possibility was ruled out when the fact was learned that there could be no purpose in capturing the *Deering*. She carried absolutely nothing to steal. Besides which, there was not the slightest sign of struggle or searching on board the ship.

The State Department entered the case to examine the chance of the schooner's being attacked by Bolshevist sympathizers. This, too, was eventually ruled out as too absurd to consider.

Whatever happened, Captain Wormell's daughter, Lulu, was persuaded her father met with attack or takeover of some kind. She could identify his handwriting in the log up to January 23rd, the day the *Deering* passed the Cape Fear

Lightship. The subsequent entries were made in a different hand.

Why? Was the captain ill in his cabin below? Or had he been abducted for some strange reason? Had he been murdered? Lulu Wormell felt he had. And possibly, also, the entire crew. The men seen by the Cape Lookout Lightship were probably the attackers!

But there were these same angles constantly cropping up: for what purpose would any kind of attack have taken place? Nothing substantiated such a possibility. The captain of the *Deering* was renowned for his good relationship with his men. He was highly popular. Why would there have been any mutiny?

As stated before, for what purpose would pirates of any type or kind take over a cargoless ship? Why, even if they had, were there not any signs of struggle?

And, as the Coast Guard pointed out, old hands at searching shores, there would have to be some signs left after a takeover of a ship. There would have to be some remnants in the form of wreckage or bodies. In this case, there wasn't a vestige of anything found at any cove or stretch of sand along the coast. The search squads had combed the coastal area for well over two months turning up precisely *nothing*.

Another theory eventually forged to the front. Could it have been that the entire crew and the officers of the *Deering* found they had contracted an incurable tropical disease while in the West Indies and decided to a man to commit mass suicide? In fact, was the strange coincidence of *two* captains complaining of illness a factor?

This was a different angle, but it, too, had

flaws. If such had been the case, then why were the lifeboats missing? And still, the puzzle remained, why were no bodies found? Any kind of suicide would have left clues.

Then came up a theory that seemed remote but still a possibility. The men of the *Deering* might have abandoned ship—though why, no one could venture a guess—and were picked up by a passing vessel, which, in turn, disappeared!

Well, there was a ship, the steel steamer *Hewitt*, carrying a cargo of sulphur from Sabine, Texas, on January 20, of that same year to Boston and Portland. She was sighted off the coast of Florida a few days later, but that was the last ever seen of her. She disappeared without leaving a trace. Not a single piece of rail or sail or body relating to her was ever found!

But there was a suggestion as to what might have happened to her: sometime in early February of '21 residents along the New Jersey coast saw a brilliant flash of light in the sea followed by high pillars of smoke. The suggestion presented itself that the *Hewitt* might have exploded with its deadly cargo of sulphur and that it did so with the crew and officers of the *Deering* aboard.

Even if such a remote occurrence had been the answer, why were there no telltale signs of such an incident? Once again, there could be found not a single piece of ship's spar or rope or crew's clothing or bodies. A seeming impossibility, even after the most destructive explosions at sea.

Another interesting sidelight unfolded relating to the *Deering*. During the investigation, the commission learned from the captain of the Cape Lookout Lightship that shortly after the strange incident with the hailing man on the deck of the *Deering* as she passed, another vessel hove into sight.

Unable to ascertain her name, the lightship flagged her an emergency signal, "Have important message." He wanted to advise her of the *Deering's* news of no anchors. The code he used was an international one. In addition to his flagging, the lightship's captain blew his No. 12 chime whistle. It is a particularly penetrating one and can be heard for a distance of five miles. Under such circumstances it is an understood law of the seas for a ship to stop and respond. This swiftly sailing vessel, contrary to all law and courtesy ignored the signalling, responded nothing and went ripping past without a suggestion of heeding the distress signal.

Who was she?

No investigation was ever able to uncover that.

It seemed the deeper probed the commissions, the deeper became the mystery. Although fraudulent clues popped up, like a so-called message in a bottle from a crew member of the *Deering,* they were all easily disproved and the search pushed harder.

All of which netted nothing for recorded history. Absolutely not one conclusive answer could be arrived at as to the fate of the *Carroll A. Deering* and its men.

What ever occurred to the men, no one will ever know. They apparently joined their fellow vanished beings of the past in the troubled Triangle Zone.

But we do know what became of the ship itself. She became quite a literal ghost ship. Residents along the coast of North Carolina in the vicinity of the Diamond Shoals declared the battered remnants of the *Deering* hulk, long months afterward, was haunted. One could plainly hear the anguished cries of the spirits roaming her deserted cabins and deck.

The Coast Guard finally decided to blow up the tormented remains of the vessel. But nature saved them the bother. A sudden storm arose one night off Cape Hatteras and smashed the derelict ship to pieces. By the next morning there was nothing left on the cleanly-swept sea coast but dislodged seagulls who had nested in her timbers for so long, howling and screeching as they circled, looking for their lost shelter from the world.

They never found it. Nor has the world of men ever located the phantom vessel's vanished crew . . . gone into the unknown depths of a mysterious zone as elusive as their story.

Chapter Seven

Quite frankly, we don't know what is happening in this so-called Bermuda Triangle. All we can do about these unexplainable disappearances is speculate.

Spokesman for the Coast Guard's
Search and Rescue Branch

SKY TRAP, TOO!

It was right after the close of World War II that the Bermuda Danger Zone began to strike out with real force. The world started to sit up and take notice. In an age when ship-to-shore radio contact made mysterious disappearances of craft of any kind a near impossibility, the impossible was happening.

And for the first time, a new aspect to the hazardous area opened up: the suggestion that the risks lurking there were not simply aquatic but atmospheric also!

The puzzle was acquiring new dimensions!

It was at a Naval base in Florida that the first such irregular puzzle piece was carved out of material that was as harmless as any nature ever had to work with: a clear day with only the mildest of winds.

The personnel at the NAAS Cecil Field in Jacksonville on that summer day of 1945 sensed nothing irregular as they went about their rounds of duties. Twenty four of them were preparing for the customary daily Overwater Navigational Flight that was to take place that afternoon.

Cecil Field was a training base instructing

pilots in dive bombing. The men were, however, not novices. They were all qualified pilots there to learn the additional "skills" of how to drop bombs.

The planes used in the operational training program were the SBD Dauntless and subsequently, the SB2C Hell Divers. The base's total craft numbered about 250 bombers. The procedure plan entailed a daily flight by a squadron of twelve planes covering some 100 mile radius in a time schedule of about two hours.

Ten of the squadron's planes were piloted by students; two by instructors. Each plane held two men: a pilot and a bomber-radioman. On such Overwater Flights, the craft dispersed after take-off, each taking an assigned course.

It was the early hours of afternoon when the twelve bombers winged upwards into the sky over Florida and swept off into the blue distance. Each craft had its crew of two, both of whom wore the customary Mae West lifepreserver. All the planes were equipped with life rafts. All of them had been pre-flight tested. None had a hint of trouble.

As the hours passed by no one at the base or in the control tower gave the training flight any concerned thought. Although not a word was received by the tower personnel from the radios of any of the planes signifying distress of any kind, the silence was not unusual. It was not base procedure to keep in radio contact with the navigational flights.

What *was* unusual was the return a few hours later, not of twelve planes, but of ten!

The men at Cecil Field scanned the skies awaiting the roar of the two missing bombers. It never came. Unbelieving that there could have been any problem, the returned ten plane crews said there had been no untoward weather conditions and no radio messages within the squadron relaying any suggestions of mechanical failures, physical illness or atmospheric difficulties from the pilots of the missing craft.

Within no time, a search was on. An area far beyond the 100 mile flight radius was covered by scores of ships and planes combing the waters between Florida, the Bermuda Islands and the West Indies.

Not a sign of the vanished planes could be spotted. There couldn't be found a trace of a life belt or boat nor a single piece of airplane wreckage. Unable to explain what could have happened, the Navy shook its collective head in astonishment and went on training somewhat unnerved students in the more understandable facts of dive bombing.

In the months that followed, the strange incident of the vanished planes began to slip into faded memory. The hashing and re-hashing of a multitude of theories about what might have happened gradually diminished in the mess hall and barracks bull sessions.

But the quiet on the Eastern United States Front was not to last long.

In December of that same year, a drama was to emerge from another Naval Air Base in Florida that not only out-did the Jacksonville mystery but every fictional thriller that ever flashed across a Hollywood screen.

It was an incident that is now known as the Lost Patrol Mystery.

The setting for this true-life drama was the Fort Lauderdale Naval Air Station. (Now the Hollywood-Fort Lauderdale International Airport). Here, too, qualified pilots were trained in bombing procedures. Every one of them was well experienced, having racked up between 350 and 400 hours of flight time, of which at least 55 were in TBM Avenger Torpedo Bombers, the type used at Fort Lauderdale on its Overwater Navigational Training Flights.

The Avenger was one of the largest and most capable single engine propeller planes ever constructed. Its wing span was over 52 feet and its power was handled by a 1600 horse power Wright cyclone engine. The craft could attain a speed of nearly 300 mph and could carry a torpedo load of some 2000 pounds of bombs. In short, she was a flying power house.

Each plane carried a crew of three; a pilot, a radioman and a gunner. For the mission scheduled for December 5th, the flight leader's plane was to carry only two men, while the remaining four bore three men each. All fourteen men involved in that now-famous Flight 19 had a lot of navigational flight experience ranging from 13 months to six years. All of the men had studied their flight plan thoroughly; knew they were to make a triangular patrol flying due east for 160 miles; then north for 40 miles; then back in a southwesterly direction to the base.

It was all very routine.

As the day scheduled for the flight dawned—it was a Wednesday—a bank of clouds plodded across Florida from west to east. Sweeping heavily in from the Gulf, the blanket of grey shrouded an area from Sarasota northwards to Tarpon Springs. In less than three hours the cloud cover was smothering the air over the Atlantic Coast from Melbourne Beach to Daytona Beach.

But as the afternoon approached, the last of this cloud bank thinned out and dispersed over the ocean east of Cape Canaveral. Almost the whole of Florida found itself dry and clear with cool temperatures of 38° and only a flurry of surface winds about normal for that time of the year—20 knots with gusts up to 31 knots.

But the men scheduled for the fateful flight during the early morning of that Wednesday weren't giving a thought to the weather, or to the routine patrol they were to fly on. They were thinking about whether or not they'd make the first showing or the second of *What Next, Corporal Hargrave?* playing that night at the base theater. Or they were taking a few minutes off to write their families about hoping to get home for Christmas.

Three of those men were buddies and were quartered in the same barracks. They were Sergeant Robert Gallivan of Northampton, Massachusetts; Private First Class Robert Gruebel of Long Island City, New York, and Corporal Allen Kosnar of Kenosha, Wisconsin.

Just prior to the time they would have to leave their barracks and go over to the operations building for the pre-flight briefing, the three friends lay stretched out on their bunks reading and talking. After about an hour Gallivan and Gruebel got up and started pulling on their flight jackets. Kosnar swung his legs over the edge of his bunk. All he could do was sit motionless and watch the others.

In minutes the two friends were dressed and at the barracks' door. They paused, waiting for the corporal to catch up.

"You go ahead, fellas. I just don't think I'm going to go on that flight—"

The sergeant and private stared back.

Kosnar nodded at them. "I know, I know. Sounds nutty but I just don't feel I wanta go. And I don't need to—I've already done my required flight time for the month, so why should I?"

His friends couldn't answer that with anything other than a sympathetic shrug.

"So long!," they called.

"See ya!," responded Kosnar and lay back on his bed. The door slammed behind his friends.

He didn't know it then, but the corporal had just saved his own life and said a final "goodby" to his closest buddies.

The two Marine gunners strode over to the operations building. Private First Class Gruebel walked with a near jump, he was so eager to plunge into the day's scheduled plans.

Gallivan must have smiled at the other's enthusiasm.

"You sure like to fly, don't you, Yo Yo?," could easily have been the sergeant's comment as they walked across the base, for he knew well, as did all his friends, how much the eager boy loved to fly. So enthusiastic was Gruebel about getting up into a plane, his buddies had nicknamed him, "Yo Yo."

Gruebel no doubt smiled back. He sure did love to fly. Getting up in the clouds was like a trip to Heaven. And why shouldn't he feel that way? As soon as his term of enlistment expired, he was going to go to Divinity School and study to be a minister.

Gallivan often shook his head in wonderment over young Gruebel's fervor. To him, Gallivan, it was all just another day's job. Not a surprising way for an old pro like himself to feel. The private had been in the service less than a year. He'd been in for over three years with most of that as an aerial gunner sweating out combat duty in the Pacific.

At the operations center the two men found the others waiting, twelve Navy and Marine fliers all assigned to Flight 19.

The briefing was routine and to the point. Each man understood it thoroughly. Every one of the planes, as usual, was carefully pre-flighted. Radios, instruments—all checked. Fuel load was to capacity, enough for over a 1000 miles.

By 1:30 p.m., the five pilots and their crews were reporting to the flight line. At 2 p.m. the first plane took off, followed by the other four. Soon all five were roaring in the wide skies above. They winged out above the Atlantic towards the wreck of a cargo ship just south of Bimini. After a series of mock torpedo runs over the concrete hulk, Flight 19 regrouped and flew onwards to fulfill their day's mission . . . and their strange destiny.

These are the last known facts about the doomed patrol.

Far away below, Allen Kosnar performed some duties then retired to the barracks' Day Room to write a letter to his folks. A while later he stashed the pages of notepaper into an envelope and licked it closed. He looked at his wrist watch. It was 3:45. Gallivan and Gruebel would be landing in another fifteen minutes.

In the Fort Lauderdale tower, a radioman was also checking his watch. Nearly 4 p.m. Almost time to turn over his duty to a relief man. He looked over the day's log in a final check.

Suddenly, he heard a frantic message come over the waves.

"Calling tower . . . this is an emergency . . . we seem to be off course . . . we cannot see land . . . repeat . . . we cannot see land . . ."

It was Lieutenant Charles Taylor, the six-year veteran in command of Flight 19.

The tower radioed back: "What is your position?"

"We are not sure . . . ," answered Taylor, . . . "We seem to be lost . . ."

The base operators stared at each other in amazement. How could experienced crews be lost under good flying conditions?

"Assume bearing due west," directed the tower.

The reply was startling.

"We cannot be sure which way is west . . . everything is wrong . . . strange . . . we cannot be sure of any direction . . . even the ocean doesn't look as it should . . ."

The base personnel exchanged glances of amazement. Even if compasses were malfunctioning, it was ridiculous that none of the five planes could find west, even if they had to depend upon visual observation! The sun was by now close to the western horizon!

During the next forty minutes the tower heard the planes talking with one another. They were apparently within sight of each other but all shared the same confusion. From their frantic interchange of messages, the base personnel could see there was a growing fear and hysteria overtaking the crews.

Then with no reason given for the action, and without any warning, Lieutenant Taylor requested the pilot of the other instructor plane to take over the command. That officer was Marine Captain George Stivers.

By now news of the strange events taking place in the skies overhead had spread across the base like fire through a hayloft. Allen Kosnar ran to the radio tower. He arrived just in time to hear Captain Stivers relay the following words which, despite radio distortion, were obviously strained with fear:

"It is 1625 hours . . . we are not certain where we are . . . must be about 225 miles northeast of base . . . looks like we are . . ."

Static crackled over the air waves. Kosnar clenched his fists and leaned over the radioman's shoulder. He felt tense as electric wire. His buddies were in that plane. Gallivan and Gruebel were Stivers' crewmen. Kosnar found himself straining to catch every word that sifted along the noisy air waves.

Stivers again:

"It looks like we are entering white water. We're completely lost!"

Then silence.

Over and over again the base tried to reestablish contact. It was impossible. Nothing could be picked up. A little more than two hours and seventeen minutes had passed since takeoff. It was the last the tower was to hear from the Lost Patrol.

Some 150 miles northwards of the Fort Lauderdale base at the Banana River Naval Air Station* Lieutenant Harry Cone of Gainesville, Florida, and his crew of twelve men were just

*Now Patrick Air Force Base serving Cape Kennedy.

reporting to the operations center prepared to stand by as the "ready crew" in case of any emergency. They handled the giant Martin Mariner PBM flying boat based at Banana and held for search and rescue missions.

The Mariner had a 124-foot wing span. The huge bird was specially built for saving downed airmen. It carried every conceivable kind of rescue apparatus from self-inflating rafts to a waterproof radio transmitter which, the moment it came in contact with water, would transmit a distress call for hours. The great ship bore a fuel load more than sufficient to stay aloft for over twenty-four hours.

She was the last word in search and rescue operations.

Within a few minutes of Cone's arrival at the Banana base operations center, a tense message from the Fort Lauderdale operator came in. Flight 19 from that base was in high emergency state. It was no time before Lieutenant Cone and his twelve crewmen were in their Mariner and headed out over the Atlantic towards the last assessed position of the lost patrol.

Less than a half hour later, the Mariner's radioman flashed the word that they were approaching their goal. But they could see nothing. There was not a sign of the missing craft.

A few minutes afterwards, the flying boat called in again. They re-stated their position and the fact that they could find nothing.

The great plane then broke contact. There was nothing more for endless minutes but complete silence.

Kosnar paced the floor in the tower room. He kept telling himself that there wasn't much to worry about. Of course, there was no float ability in the Avenger—once it hit the water, it would sink like a rock, but the men were experienced in handling that and in ditching procedures. They knew well how to use their life rafts in fast sea-escape action. They'd make it.

As for the Big Ship—there wasn't anything the Mariner couldn't handle in sea search and rescue! It could land like a gull on the roughest sea and she was manned by a crew of thirteen men that knew their business like nobody's business!

Why wasn't the Mariner checking in again by now?

Kosnar licked nervous lips and paused behind one of the operators desperately trying to pick up the huge plane on the air waves. Over and over the operator tried. It was useless. All attempts failed. He sat back and shook his head. There was nothing. Only silence.

The corporal swallowed hard. How could it be? How could a giant plane built to handle any emergency be so completely gone, too! But it was. To the whole tower personnel it was now clear that the Navy Air Force was now missing six planes instead of five!

The Fort Lauderdale tower called for help to Naval headquarters and to the local Coast Guard. Immediately ships and planes were combing the nearby waters and beaches. Nothing turned up. Only night.

"FT. . . . . FT. . . . ."

The operator hunched over his set in excitement. These were part of Flight 19's call letters! Could one of the Avengers still be aloft? How could that be possible? The last plane in the squadron would have run out of fuel some two hours before! Yet, no other plane would have used those letters. . . .

He kept calling. Tried over and over to make contact with that weak signal. It was useless.

All through the long night of December 5th, the Coast Guard searched avidly. By dawn the aircraft carrier *Solomons* had moved into the area and was dispatching her load of planes to join in the hunt. Overhead, in a tight grid-search pattern, over 300 planes aided. Twelve land parties did their best by combing every inch of shoreline from St. Augustine in the north to Miami in the south. The Everglades were covered as was the Gulf of Mexico. Even the British RAF from the Bahamas lent their assistance. Absolutely nothing was found.

Not one of the search organizations was able to turn up a single piece of evidence. There was not found a small item of personal clothing or remnant of bodies. Not a sign of a flare or a life raft. There was not a piece of wreckage or a suggestion of an oil slick. Nothing.

A Naval Board of Inquiry was set up. After long weeks of investigation, the group were able to ascertain not one concrete intelligent idea of what could have occurred. Their summation was brief:

"We are not able to even make a good guess as to what happened."

Later, one of that board's members was quoted as saying, "They vanished as completely as if they'd flown to Mars!"

For many months following, the Florida bases were consumed with talk about the mysterious flights. It seemed an incredible possibility that out of all those craft and the many experienced men on them not *one* had survived! How

could anything have happened that would practically *simultaneously* and *entirely* obliterate
everything! Even the worst of air crashes and
sea disasters leave some floating debris. Even
if one had blown up, it would have left evidence. And could all six have exploded?

The one common answer every thoughtful
analysis produced was really no answer at all,
but it was an interesting observation: the difficulty with all of the planes seemed not to arise
from a mechanical or physical problem—or even
the weather—not one radio message suggested
that it was. The trouble seemed to be related to
a *confusion as to direction.*

What could that mean?

There were no solutions forthcoming. Not
then; not now. The incident of the Lost Patrol
and its Rescue Ship has gone down in history
as an unsolved riddle. The strange occurrence
has become a legend in its own time.

To Allen Kosnar it became more than a fascinating story; it was a painful remembrance.

In 1969, twenty-four years after the sad event,
the lone buddy returned to the scene where the
whole tragedy started. He went back to Fort
Lauderdale Airport to aid in the filming of a
documentary. He stared at the old barracks
where once, long ago, he had lain back on his
bunk with a wave and heard a "So long!," from
two men who'd been his closest pals. Never did
he dream at that moment, the time would be,
indeed, for "so long!"

But the Sky-Trap was not closed for ever after
the vanished patrol incident. Just short of 26
months later, on January 29, 1948, it opened
again! This time it swallowed up a commercial

craft. And it repeated the performance twice within a little over a year's time!

The *Star Tiger*, a big four-engined luxury airliner belonging to the British South American Airways Company (BSAAC) carrying 22 passengers and a crew of six, swept majestically through the skies on January 29th, 1948. She was en route to Havana from London with stops along the way at the Azores and Hamilton, Bermuda.

Leaving her first stop well behind her, the huge craft headed into strong winds towards the second leg of her trip, Bermuda.

It was slow going. At 10:30 p.m., the plane's Captain David Colby reported by radio to the Bermuda tower that he anticipated arriving at Hamilton an hour and a half late.

At one o'clock in the morning he radioed again, stating that he was approximately 440 miles northeast of Bermuda and still bucking strong winds. Other than stout winds he made no mention of any kind of real difficulty. The skies were clear and there appeared to be no mechanical problems of any kind.

But something must have gone wrong shortly after that last message. The Bermuda tower could not establish radio contact with the plane again. It never arrived. Again, air-sea rescue units were quickly pressed into service. But not a scrap of evidence was discovered.

Months of exhaustive inquiry netted exactly nothing. Ultimately, only one conclusion was forthcoming in regards to the mysterious disappearance of one of England's proudest planes: "It may truly be said," as one report worded it, "that no more baffling problem has ever been presented for investigation."

But the Bermuda Mystery Zone wasn't finished yet. Not by a long wingspan!

Almost exactly eleven months later, the skytrap opened again. It gobbled up just about the happiest cargo ever flown through that area: a chartered plane flying a load of holiday merrymakers. Thirty men and women and two babies —32 passengers in all—were still in festive spirits from a wonderful Christmas in Puerto Rico. They had boarded the craft at San Juan around 10 p.m. and the stalwart DC-3 took off with a roar into clear, velvety skies.

Shortly after 1 a.m. the plane's Captain Robert Linquist radioed his position. It was picked up at Kingston, Jamaica. At a little after 4 a.m., the pilot sent another position report: he was fifty miles south of Miami. The message was filled with nothing but ease and contentment. Some of the passengers were awake and singing Christmas carols. In sight of land and close to his destination, Linquist asked for landing instructions. He got them. But no one knows whether or not he ever received them, for not another word was ever heard again from the craft. It simply vanished without cause or trace.

In spite of intensive searching—over 310,000 miles of sea and land—not a sign as to the fate of the DC-3 was ever found.

Only a little over a month after that strange and inexplicable incident, the Mystery Zone made itself felt again in the innocent skies of the area. A huge BSAAC airliner, the *Star Ariel* —sister ship of the ill-fated *Star Tiger*—took off from the Bermuda airport at 7:45 a.m. and winged into a perfect powder-blue sky. She was headed for Santiago, Chile with a stop due at Kingston, Jamaica. The craft carried thirteen passengers and seven crew members under the command of Captain J. C. McPhee. The *Ariel* had been carefully checked at Bermuda just prior to take-off and as an extra safety measure had had her reserve tanks filled with fuel—enough to give the plane an extra ten hours of flight time, if needed.

She was to need something far more than fuel, it would seem.

At 8:25 the Bermuda tower received a routine report: "This is Captain McPhee aboard the *Ariel* en route to Kingston, Jamaica from Bermuda. We have reached cruising altitude. Fair weather. Expected time of arrival Kingston as scheduled."

With those words, Captain McPhee broke off radio contact. It was the last ever heard from him. The *Ariel* joined its sister ship in that strange Bermuda realm of thin and vanquishing air!

A U.S. Navy task force on maneuvers thereabouts, turned in with a vim to search for the missing craft. It sent its aircraft carriers, cruisers and destroyers to scan the waters.

Nothing.

The two sister ships had vanished in the same area only a few hundred miles of each other and in less than a year's time!

In the early 1950's the firm of British South American Airways Company (BSAAC) was absorbed by the British Overseas Airways Corporation (BOAC) and in the merger the records relating to the strange disappearances of the *Star Tiger* and *Star Ariel* were turned over to the British Ministry of Aviation in London.

The Ministry of Aviation dedicated itself to unraveling the puzzle of the two completely obliterated airplanes. It investigated each incident as intensely as the U.S. Navy's Board of Inquiry had studied the mystery of the Lost Patrol and its would-be rescuers. The conclusions reached in England were practically identical to the U.S. Navy Board's: the planes had disappeared and must be presumed lost at sea, though no evidence had ever been found to substantiate this theory.

The losses of the two British airliners resulted in the withdrawal of that type of craft from overseas passenger service although the *Tudor IV* had operated successfully in other areas of the world. Nothing was found to indicate any defect related to the craft itself. There was nothing wrong with the equipment; the pilots; the communications; the weather or the meteorological conditions at the time of the incidents.

What was enveloping aircraft in that one small area of the mid-Atlantic ocean?

No one had an answer.

In the years subsequent to these mysterious and utterly baffling phenomena, many more planes followed suit. Among them was the inexplicable disappearance of a giant Air Force tanker that took off from Langley Air Force Base in Virginia headed for the Azores in January of 1962. About a quarter of an hour later, the control tower at the base picked up a flow of indecipherable signals from that ship indicating it was having directional problems.

Then radio contact broke off. There was nothing but silence. That was the end of any communication from the tanker. The usual exhaustive search brought no clue of what the tragedy had been.

The airfield at Nassau in the Bahamas reported a similar freak instance in that same year. On a perfectly clear day when any pilot could have known his position, on instruments or not, a private plane approaching from north asked for guidance.

The Nassau tower gave him the requested instructions. But instead of easily advancing on them, at a time and under conditions when the island must have been clearly visible, the pilot seemed utterly unable to grasp them. He kept repeating his requests for directional aid. Later, the operator was quoted as saying the plane's pilot behaved as though he were descending in a pea-soup fog rather than on a sunny day!

After long minutes of confused dialogue, during which time the man was never able to respond to the tower with any clarity as to his position, suddenly the radio contact was cut off. Nothing more from the pilot came through. *He* was never seen or heard from again.

The years following brought further vanishings with no explanations: a U.S. super-fortress and a British army transport plane. On other occasions, two U.S. Navy patrol planes flew off into the air south of Florida and were never heard from again nor could any trace of them be discovered. The usual lack of debris, life-belts, bodies, oil slick or calls of distress from any of them. All of them in the fairest of weather had simply, like all their predecessors, been in some way, "swallowed up" in a strange void, leaving no sign or fragment of evidence as to what could have happened to them.

As with the many vessels that had sailed into oblivion in this weirdest of areas in the world, many airplanes apparently have taken off and flown through some invisible "doorway" in the sky which, it seems, opens only one way. Once men have discovered it, they can never return to tell about it.

Chapter Eight

> ... upon the watery plain
> The wrecks are all thy deed, nor doth
>   remain
> A shadow of man's ravage, save his own,
> When for a moment, like a drop of rain,
> He sinks into thy depths with bubbling
>   groan,
> Without a grave, unknelled, uncoffined and
>   unknown.
>
> Lord Byron, *Childe Harold's Pilgrimage*

THE WORLD'S
OTHER TRIANGLES

In recent years, as the Bermuda Triangle has been absorbing the attention of questioning minds, both scientific and unscientific, another enigmatic zone in our world has been settling into focus: the area of Pacific Ocean that stretches between Japan and the Marianas Islands.

It too, has seen strange disappearances that parallel those of the Bermuda Triangle.

To Japan, the mysteries related to this area are nothing new. Ask any fisherman of those waters and he will nod and tell you, "Of course, everybody knows the fishing is wondrous but the dangers are terrible. At any time, the monsters who dwell down there may rise up and swallow you and your boat and your fine catch all up and nothing will be left of you to carry back to your village."

If the explanation has varied from the monster theme, it has switched only to the concept of an equally hostile corps of demons who live below the churning waters of the "Devil's Sea."

So for centuries this unpredictable area of ocean has held fearful sway over Japanese villagers. But scientists have always known better than the suffering fishermen of the past. It is not devils or underwater creatures but the famous Fuji Volcanic Zone that causes the frightful "seaquakes."

This volcanic band runs via the Izu Peninsula southwards into the Pacific as far as the Mariana Islands. Its above sea-level portions form the cores of many islands including the largest, Iwo Jima. When the underwater portions of volcanic cones erupt, then the sea explodes and creates the dreaded "tsunami"—a towering wave of about 200 feet in height that sweeps everything before it into destruction.

It has always been the eruption of these underwater volcanos and the accompanying *tsunami*, say the Japanese scientists, that have for centuries destroyed shipping and wiped out tiny fishing crafts.

But, as with the Bermuda Triangle case histories, there are many unexplained factors that enter into the disappearances in these waters and the Japanese are frank to admit they have no conclusive answers.

Take the year 1952. On September 18th a fishing vessel, the *Eleventh Myojin Maru*, returned to port with the story that the sea had "raised up into a large dome" in the waters to the east of the Bayonnaise Islands! Immediately, several scientific organizations sprang into action to investigate.

Within three days time, the Marine Safety Bureau had dispatched its coastal patrol ship, the S.S. *Shikine* to the Devil's Sea and the *Tokyo University of Fisheries and Earthquake* had organized a researching party to undertake the mission of checking out the reports at close hand. The research party was a list of real scientific minds representing the *Tokyo University of Fisheries and Earthquake;* the *Research Institute of Tokyo University;* the *Tokyo University of Education;* the *Tokyo Science Museum;* the *Bureau of Fisheries* as well as reporters from the Asahi Press.

By the 23rd of September the party aboard the ship, the S.S. *Shinyo Maru,* was instrument-deep in the dramatic experience of seeing a volcano exploding in the depths of the Devil's Sea about 4.6 nautical miles north-eastwards from the Bayonnaise Island.

Meanwhile the Marine Bureau's vessel had returned to port and reported the existence of a new rock bank at the site of the eruption spouting yellow vapor. This bank had slipped somewhat underwater by the time the second research ship, the *Shinyo Maru* reached the site and only two projections of rock were above sea-level at that time, due to continuing eruptions.

Based on the reports of these two vessels, as they radioed in, the Hydrographic Bureau lost no time in issuing a name to the newly-discovered volcano: *Myojin-sho.*

On the 23rd of September, the *Shinyo Maru* turned about and headed for home. The eruptions were increasingly violent. By the next day, she, like the *Shikine,* was safely back at port.

But the Hydrographic Bureau, meanwhile, had also sent out one of its patrol ships to investigate. After checking the reports of the two returning ships on the 23rd and 24th, she began to grow concerned over her own vessel, the *Fifth Kaiyo-Maru.* She was carrying an impressive research party and had pulled out of Tokyo on September 21st. For days the Bureau awaited word. It was a matter of great concern, for this ship held some of the nation's foremost scientists. A total of 31 people including geologists, oceanographers, captain and crew members.

By the 24th there was still no word from the research ship. A most unusual circumstance to have received not a single radio message from her since she'd left port. The other two vessels returned, bearing no news of the lost Bureau ship. They had stayed long enough to see *Myojin-sho* in action and that was all. Then they'd set a course for home. There had been no sight of the *Fifth Kaiyo-Maru*.

The Hydrographic Bureau reported the craft as missing and the search was on. Every inch of the Devil's Sea was covered. Scores of ships equipped with life-saving devices plus numerous aircraft spun out over the area, combing the ocean for some evidence of the vanished vessel. There was scarcely a sign to be uncovered. Not a life-preserver nor a life raft was spotted. Not a single personal item such as a piece of clothing was found.

There were fragments of debris floating in the area of *Myojin-sho* which one of the rescuing ships picked up and took back to the lab. The pieces were identified as wood belonging to the lost ship and they bore the only slim evidence that was ever to be found: pumice flakes were clinging to them . . . tiny particles of volcanic substance that tallied with the rock specimens gathered from *Myojin-sho*.

On the basis of that evidence, a Fact-Finding Board set up by the Japanese government to investigate the mysterious disappearance issued, after long deliberation, its final conclusion: the *Fifth Kaiyo-Maru* was evidently overturned, sunk and destroyed completely on September 24th, 1952 after an explosion of the submarine volcano of *Myojin-sho*.

The nation mourned the loss of that research party and its crew who so courageously set forth to forward man's knowledge. They were a hard core of well-known scientific minds. They are still missed. Dr. Hiroshi Niino, a professor with the *Tokyo University of Fisheries and Earthquake*, wrote recently of that tragedy:

"The great sacrifice of the scientists and crew who so willingly undertook the dangerous cruise will live throughout the history. Their sacrifice left a great gap in the men of science of Japan, but it is to them that a new page has been opened in the science of the sea."

Does that "new page" open to a solution to the Triangle-type mystery?

No answers so far. Although the Japanese government has declared the Devil's Sea a Danger Zone, it has gotten no closer to facts.

One Japanese organization concerned with what those possible facts could be, is the *Science and Technology Agency* of Tokyo. They are still dealing with several questions which loom large in the unsolved vanishing of the famous research ship along with others before.

Why were there no communications from the troubled ship? Although it had two good radio apparatuses, neither was used. There had never been a single call of distress or intimation from the radio operator that there was trouble of any kind . . . or expected problems whatsoever.

Why were there no dead bodies found? Even after the most violent underwater eruptions, some bit of human remains will be ultimately found risen to the surface. Not a stitch or snip of anything was uncovered.

And most mysterious of all, why were there no traces of floating oil? Such a circumstance seems hardly possible in the case of the *Fifth Kaiyo-Maru* which was carrying 30 tons of oil on board!

So it is, that the foregoing still points up, as one agent of the *Science Agency's Marine Development Division* put it, "many matters left unknown."

As with the Bermuda Triangle, the problems centering on the puzzling area go much higher than any underwater deadlines. The sky, too, seems to be involved.

No less a personage than Arthur Godfrey can testify to that. On his "Round the World Tour" in his two-engined jet a few years ago (it was widely covered in the press) he had an experience he will tell you that he will never forget. Just as he got over the Devil's Sea area, zap!, everything on his instrument panel went off! His radio, compasses, gas gauge, etc. went completely dead for nearly an hour. "When you've got only four hours' worth of gas," he reported later, "that's not nice!" Once out of the area, everything shot back into action again. Not a former believer in Triangles or any such things, the incident changed his mind and he told the world so later on a television show.

In recent years, according to a report in a May 1971 issue of the *Bermuda Royal Gazette*, four other pilots since Godfrey related they, too, in flying from Japan experienced a complete radio blackout for one and a half hours. Later the instruments started functioning again and they were set on the right course, though they never knew how they got there!

After Godfrey's experience, research on the "Devil's Triangle" pushed harder. One of those private investigative agencies was the *Society for the Investigation of the Unexplained of New Jersey* founded by scientist, Ivan Sanderson. That group unearthed that during World War II both Japanese and U. S. military planes had plotted the Devil Sea. Its shape turned out to be a kind of "blob" that is pitched at an angle of about 25 degrees SW to NS. A very interesting fact, determined the Society, since it compares almost exactly in size and "pitch" to the Bermuda Triangle!

Setting out, then, to examine other mysterious regions of vanishings all over the world, and measuring their positions the Society (consisting of mathematicians, geographers, geodists and electromagnetic engineers among others) came up with this intriguing theory.

There appear to be *ten* equally-spaced "blobs," "lozenges," "triangles" or "diamond-shaped" areas, however one wishes to define them, covering the face of the globe which occur at exactly 72-degree intervals, five in the Northern Hemisphere and five in the Southern!

As this group measured them out, they are, in addition to the Bermuda zone and the Devil's Sea: the western Mediterranean; northeast of the Hawaiian Islands in the Northern Pacific; off the southeast coast of Argentina; off the southeast coast of South Africa; the Tasman Sea off Australia; the east Indian Ocean; western area of the Indian Ocean off the southwestern coast of Australia, and one unique region of "land-deadliness"—Afghanistan.

If these investigators are right, then our earth is spanned by a very precise trigonometrical grid of equilateral triangles, all equidistant from each other. If one includes the two Poles, the network incorporates twelve mysterious zones that involve unexplained disappearances.

But can this be all the problem, so neatly packaged? Many investigators feel that it is not all-inclusive. What of the many unsolved vanishings of planes over lands, other than Afghanistan, such as those over the Sahara Desert during and after World War II? The Gulf of Mexico, too, though not lining up into position on any network of zones, has had its full share of mysterious incidents.

So far, no one has come up with the perfect answer, but many are trying. From the Science and Technology Agencies of Japan to several investigative commissions in the United States, many are trying. And whatever they come up with, and whenever, the world will be listening.

Chapter Nine

Scorpion-fish: *member of a large family
(Scorpaenidae) of carnivorous fish inhab-
iting all seas and especially abundant in
tropical waters of the Pacific; also in the
West Indies. Scorpion-fish are equipped
with poisonous dorsal spines.*

Columbia Encyclopedia

IS THERE SOMETHING BELOW?

The name, "Scorpion" has long been synony-mous with a "dangerous barb." Not only as a creature of the spider class so well known to man, but also as a fish, lesser known but equally perilous. The stiff dorsal spines of the scorpion fish can inflict wounds of intense pain. If deep, the stabs can prove fatal.

In World War II the wounds inflicted by the submarine, *Scorpion*—SS 278 were just as treach-erous and damaging to mortal man. The artful sub hovered in depths and darted through shallows. She was the fifth craft of the U.S. Fleet to be named for the poisonous fish and she lived up to the killing reputation of that sea creature throughout her whole brief but active career in the Pacific during the Second World War.

The *Scorpion*—SS 278 was built at the Ports-mouth Navy Yard in New Hampshire. She was launched on July 20th, 1942 under the sponsor-ship of Miss Elizabeth Monagle, daughter of the Master Moulder at the Yard. The ship was placed in commission on October 1st of that same year and was at Pearl Harbor by March of '43.

From there she put forth on a patrol during

which she racked up an amazing record of swift attack and quick withdrawal. Boldly attacking Japanese cargo vessels under heavy convoy, she sank freighters, destroyers and heavily-armed patrol vessels deftly dodging resultant rains of depth charges.

The sub terminated her first patrol on the 8th of May in '43 and returned for rest and overhauling to Pearl Harbor.

Three weeks later, she was back in the seas. After topping off with fuel at Midway, she set her course eastward to the Formosa-Tsushima-Nagasaki shipping lanes. In this second tour, she ran into some of her heaviest action.

On the morning of July 3rd, she went to battle stations when a contact proved to be a convoy of five freighters with destroyer escort. The *Scorpion* fired salvos of five and three torpedoes with divergent spread. She soon heard five resulting explosions. Struck squarely were two cargo ships, the *Azan Maru* and the *Kokuryu Maru*.

With an enemy escort and two vessels on the beam with near zero angles, *Scorpion* did not wait to observe the results. She started down on the last shot.

Soon she was stopping screws to avoid stirring up a mud trail and was settling down quietly on the ocean bottom.

Seven close range depth charges exploded around her, rocking the sub like a toy. The men strained and waited tensely with each burst. The charges missed.

Two minutes later a chain dragged over the hull. The men listened in awesome hush as the metal cord ominously scraped the submarine.

In the next instant the dragging was followed by a close and violent depth charge.

Slowly, the *Scorpion* moved out. She decided to try for deeper water in a radical change of course.

Once again, she was caught by the chain dragging her hull and, as before, shook from the subsequent dropping of depth charges. One-two-three-four! She kept moving as the charges kept plummeting. Close, one after the other. But they missed. Gradually, the *Scorpion* edged her way into deep water and she was away and safe. She had escaped the trap.

She had sustained no real damage except for her sound gear which was completely out of commission. She was not able to make any contacts for the next three days. She then left the action area and returned to Midway on July 15th. By mid-August she was back at Pearl Harbor for completion of battle repairs. She was awarded two battle stars for outstanding bravery in action.

She was to earn a third battle star. It would also be her last.

On October 13th of 1943, the *Scorpion* cleared Pearl Harbor for another patrol. Her scanning area was to be around the Marianas Islands.

She didn't know it then (no one knew about any Mystery Zones then), but the *Scorpion* was scouting no ordinary sea. She was cutting through the depths of the Devil's Sea! She was in Japan's "Bermuda Triangle!"

In early November she crossed paths with a Japanese cruiser, which she chased in vain, losing her in a squall. But three days later on the 8th of November the action-eating sub found a series of targets. She was in a target-filled area, she found—a course that ran up the Mari-anas Group from Agrihan to Farallon de Pajaros Islands.

The scrappy sub attacked and ran from a "Q-boat"; a convoy of a freighter and tanker and subsequently near Saipan Island, caught sight of a large troop transport under the escort of two destroyers and a corvette which she ran after in a high speed chase, giving up only after her search radar went out of commission.

Later she picked up the same targets in her periscope. She quickly gave chase again until near midnight. Finally the targets became lost from sight. *Scorpion* reluctantly broke off pur-suit and returned to Pearl Harbor for refit. It was the 5th of December, 1943. Her battle rec-ord had now stashed up for her three battle stars. She was a heroine.

On December 29th, under the command of Commander M. G. Schmidt, the *Scorpion* re-turned to the seas for her fourth patrol. It was her last.

She cut back into the waters of the Devil's Sea. On the fifth day after her departure from Pearl Harbor, the *Scorpion* radioed for assist-ance. She had a man aboard with her who had sustained a fracture of the upper arm. The sub requested a rendezvous with the *Herring* who was then in the area. But rough seas prevented the *Herring* from taking the man on board and it proved impossible to take the injured crew-man to Midway for treatment.

The *Scorpion* understood. She radioed back around midnight:

"Under control."

It was the last word ever received from the fighter sub.

She was never seen or heard from again.

When no report had been received by February 24th, she was directed to make a transmission. There was no acknowledgement. Consequently, the Navy recorded the *Scorpion* assumed lost in action.

But was she?

After the close of the war, the Japanese records were carefully examined for information about the record-making sub. There was nothing. There was no tiny clue furnished as to what happened to the *Scorpion*. She had not been sunk by the enemy. The Japanese had had no confrontation with her at that time. There was nothing to be found that could tell of what her fate had been. To this day, no trace or any remains of the ship have been found, nor of her six officers and 54 enlisted men. They had all vanished in the depths of the Devil's Sea.

The *Scorpion* was gone but not forgotten. The Navy recorded her courageous action in its historic annals honoring the officers and crew who went down with her. That recognition climaxed in a namesake: the Navy's newest underwater power house built in 1958 by the Electric Boat company Division of the General Dynamics Corporation of Groton, Connecticut.

This newest (and sixth) *Scorpion*—SS (N)—589 was launched with fanfare on December 19, 1959 under the sponsorship of Mrs. Elizabeth B. Morrison, daughter of Commander Maximilian G. Schmidt, USN, commanding officer of the World War II sub which vanished in the Pacific waters.

The new nuclear-powered "fish" was commissioned at Groton, Connecticut, on July 29th,

1960. She was under the command of Commander Norman B. Bessac.

One of the most beautiful pieces of construction ever to come out from a shipyard, the new *Scorpion* was a SKIPJACK-Class nuclear powered submarine with length overall of 251-feet, 9 inches; extreme beam of 31-feet, 7 inches; surfaced displacement of 3,075 tons and a submerged displacement of 3,500 tons. Her design accommodated ten officers and 98 enlisted men. Her armament included six torpedo tubes. She was powered by one water-cooled nuclear reactor.

Scorpion was assigned to Submarine Division 62, Squadron Six, U.S. Atlantic Fleet. All through the early 1960's, the ship scored a record of achievement that won her one award after another for meritorious service.

Specializing in submarine warfare tactics in waters predominantly around Bermuda, Florida and Puerto Rico, she operated in rigorous exercises as both the hunted and the hunter. So skillful was she in aggressive imaginative opposition and so important was the data she collected during these operations to the knowledge of antisubmarine warfare readiness, she received two more awards: the Atlantic Submarine Battle Efficiency Competition Award for the fiscal year of 1963 as well as the annual award for Excellence in Torpedo Fire Control and Performance.

Once again, a US Navy *Scorpion* was a winner.

For a time.

The mid-1960's were spent by the prideful sub in trans-oceanic patrols as well as exercises off the eastern seaboard of the United States and in the Caribbean Sea. Her accomplishment of missions of high national importance resulted in another award. The Navy's Commendation Medal went to the *Scorpion's* Commanding officer, Commander James R. Lewis, in recognition of his outstanding leadership, foresight and professional skill. Other officers and men aboard the *Scorpion* were also cited for meritorious achievement. The outstanding performance and superior teamwork of the whole manpower aboard the sub resulted in the *Scorpion* receiving the Battle Efficiency Competition Award for Atlantic Submarines, for two successive years —1965 and '66.

It seemed an unbeatable combination of ship-craftsmanship, crew and officers. Until the year 1968.

The *Scorpion* had entered the Norfolk Naval Shipyard in Virginia on February 1st, 1967 for overhaul that included refueling of her nuclear reactor. She was preparing for sea trial during the coming months. By October of that year, she was ready for refresher training that took her to New London, thence south to Puerto Rico and the Virgin Islands for Weapons System Acceptance Tests. Commander Lewis had been relieved of duty as commanding officer by Commander Francis A. Slattery, U.S. Navy.

Such type training operation out of Norfolk as home base, came to an end in early 1968. On February 15th, the *Scorpion* departed on a new assignment in farther waters. She was to engage in operations with the Sixth Fleet in the Mediterranean for an extensive period. She touched Rota, Spain, in early March and reached Taranto, Italy, on March 10th.

The following months were spent throughout

the Mediterranean engaging in various highly successful operations with the Sixth Fleet.

That May the active submarine was ready for a return to her home base. She set her course for Norfolk.

They were happy days that followed.

Until the 21st day of May, at least. That was the day, the *Scorpion* broke the long silence of her training operations to contact home base.

The men were in excellent spirits. They were all eager to get back home and were looking forward to seeing their families. *Scorpion* reported her position off the Azores. All was going well. She would be home within a week.

That was the last ever heard from the nuclear sub. There was never a further word or distress call or the slightest intimation of trouble from her received from that moment on.

After the passage of nearly a week and no sign of the craft off the coast of Virginia, the Navy put out an uneasy bulletin: the *Scorpion* was "overdue."

The radio operators tried desperately and near-continuously to establish contact with the sub. Their efforts were unanswered.

For over a week intensive air and sea search was conducted. Not a sign of the craft was spotted. After nine fruitless days, the submarine was officially listed as "lost."

In Norfolk a Navy Board of Inquiry convened to try to get to the bottom of what might have happened. As is so frequently the case in such disappearances, there was nothing to go on. No distress word; no suggestion of trouble. It was a "dead end."

Months went by without a trace of the undersea craft. But modern technology came to the aid with rewarding results. Subs carried TV cameras back and forth over the ocean depths between the Azores and Norfolk, the chartered route of the *Scorpion,* photographing the Atlantic floor. On October 29th, at a depth of over 10,000 feet, the dead sub was located by the USNS *Mizar* (T-Ago-11). Her remains rested on the silt-thick bottom in the middle of the ocean, some 500 miles southwest of the Azores. In the fringe-area of the old Atlantic Danger Zone?

What had happened to her?

No one could come up with even a likely answer. The Board of Inquiry studied some 12,000 photographs of the Atlantic floor and every strewn stretch of oceanic debris the cameras picked up, but not one shot revealed a single small clue.

No cause could be determined as to what occurred to the undersea craft on its homeward course that fated May that spelled the end for nearly a hundred lives. To this day no possible cause has been reconstructed.

The mystery of the two *Scorpions* joins the long roster of previous inexplicable cases. Remarkably similar to the disappearances of the two *Wasps,* the vanishing subs have given the puzzle a new dimension:

Is there something *below* in the Atlantic's Mystery Zone as well as *on* and *over* the surface of the water?

A new twist to the Bermuda Triangle was added. And the whole strange eerie area burst onto the consciousness of man with renewed vigor. What *was* going on?

From the time of the nuclear sub's mysterious disappearance in 1968 investigative organizations, scientists, writers, the curious, the adventurous and whom-will-you have launched into an interest in the Mystery Zone that has nearly set the whole world on its ear.

Few subjects today elicit more interest and curiosity than does the question of this area.

"What," thousands of concerned people today are asking, "is going on in the Bermuda Triangle?" The area is a zone of disaster or deadliness!

Why?

There are numerous possible explanations.

The theories are not answers. They are suggestions and/or opinions. None of them are conclusive. But they are provocative, mindstretching, and, every one of them, worthy of consideration.

Let us, in the final chapter, examine those that have been presented.

Chapter Ten

The causes of things are ever more inter-
esting than the events themselves.

Cicero, *Letters to Atticus*

WHAT HAPPENED
TO EVERYBODY?

The query, "What happened to everybody?" is being asked more repeatedly by more people all over the world today in connection with the Bermuda Triangle disappearances.

Of course, there are, as yet, no conclusive answers. But there are speculations and they abound.

Not infrequently, especially when normal laws will not provide an answer, the world of psychic insight does. One of the first solutions, presented about the Triangle Zone Mystery came from the "Third Eye" of a Connecticut psychic named Ed Snedeker.

Snedeker will tell you, he knows well where everybody went in the Triangle Twilight Zone. He has been "in touch" with them.

There are numerous funnels or tunnels in our atmosphere, declares Snedeker, that are invisible to the human eye but which exist nonetheless as imprisoning "sleeves," so to speak. He, himself, has seen them physically and they contain the vanished people and craft of the Triangle area.

Shaped somewhat like tornado funnels, these atmospheric "sleeves" have sucked up various people and vessels over the years and then, continuing to spiral with their prey in their grasp, these whirling forms move in a course from North to South, finally depositing their contents, both human and inert, in the vicinity of the Antarctic or possibly *beyond*.

This Connecticut psychic not only has "seen" them but has "talked" with some of them. "Although they are not visible and will never be seen on this Earth again, they are present and their voices can be heard," asserts Snedeker.

"One man I 'contacted' was an RAF pilot who got into this Triangle mess around 1945 and was unheard of for many years. He was around 50 years old at the time he vanished. When I searched for him and found him in 1969 he was still alive. Know where he was? Somewhere down within the hollow of the Earth!"

Along these same mystic lines, a learned Tibetan Lama, Lobsang Rampa, has offered the world a solution to the disappearances in the Mystery Zone. He tells us that the planes and ships went from this world to another world of anti-matter.

Rampa maintains that there exists in the Universe a world of anti-matter just as there is this world of matter we know. "Everyone and everything on Earth," he reports, "has a counterpart of the opposite polarity in another galaxy in another system of time altogether." He explains that the Triangle disappearances are due to a "split" in one world coming into close juxtaposition with a "split" in our world, as they move through space, causing men and craft to "jump" from this world into the opposite one's "opening."

Along the lines of more physical science

rather than psychic search, investigation is going on just as intently.

Individuals, organizations, institutions and many researchers have emerged with one common conclusion that at least narrows the choice of possible causes: the basis of trouble in the Mystery Zone is not the age-old, havoc-creating atmospheric or oceanic foul-weather reasons that ordinarily are responsible for sinkings and downings of craft. In the various Triangle cases such causes were almost universally not present.

One outstanding factor common to most craft at the time of their disappearances was the presence of good weather.

Of course, there are no logs remaining from ships that vanished, for their records disappeared along with the men and the vessels, but racking up data accumulated in our era of ship-to-shore radio it is easily seen that in nearly every case of vanishing craft, its radio contact just prior to the disappearance either made no comment about a problem with weather or specifically stated that the conditions were good.

Typical of such circumstances are the final words received from Captain McPhee aboard the *Star Ariel* en route from Bermuda to Jamaica in January of 1949. As we have noted, he checked in to the Bermuda tower with the message: . . . "We have reached cruising altitude. Fair weather. Expected time of arrival Kingston as scheduled." And that was the end.

So, the basis of the strange problem of the Triangle is not just plain old-fashioned bad weather.

Nor does it lie in such ocean phenomena as giant waves rising upwards from a storm center; "seaquakes" (the underwater equivalent to earthquakes); or violent ocean currents, since vessels in the Triangle Mystery are known to have been largely in good weather circumstances and not involved with such treacherous waters; nor would freak ocean conditions affect aircraft.

The effect seems not to relate to storm weather, air turbulence, air or ocean currents or the usual problematical aquatic or atmospheric conditions of any kind. It seems rather an environmental puzzle—the key to which man has not yet unlocked.

Thinking men are seriously questioning: is there an overall influence in the Triangle area that affects a craft whether it be *on* the water; *over* it or *under* it?

The Navy, according to a representative of that branch of the Armed Services, is trying to get to the solution through a plan called, "Project Magnet." This investigation is centered on the possibility of electromagnetic gravitational and atmospheric disturbances that might be responsible for literally disintegrating craft. It is noteworthy that on the day of the vanishing Avengers in the Lost Patrol, a ship in the area reported seeing a large ball of fire in the skies. It is highly unlikely that all five planes could have collided—joined by a sixth—when the craft, judging by their radio conversations, were all in sight of each other. But it is possible that a fireball in the atmosphere could have been created by the impact of the patrol and its rescue ship with a disintegrating electromagnetic force.

The Office of Naval Research a few years ago supported studies in such speculations by issuing a grant to Dr. John Caristoiu, the renowned geophysicist. Caristoiu concluded his intensive research with the publication of a paper entitled, "The Two Gravitational Fields and Gravitational Waves Propagation."

In his work, Dr. Caristoiu contends from a purely mathematical basis that there might exist, particularly over marine areas, some sort of gravitic force different and separate from gravity as we know it . . . a kind of second gravity. Such a force might exert effects on the earth's surface or ocean surface—as well as *over* it and *under* it—that are wholly different from regular gravity. Such previous unknown efffects, he feels, might be easily detected in this day and age by our present highly developed techniques for exploring the physical nature of our planet.

Other scientists also are deep in studies of possible magnetic peculiarities and their patterns of dispersement over our globe.

These scientists suggest that there is only one gravity force but that there occur from time to time certain aberrations in its normal effect of attraction. Could there be, for example, a field of ordinary gravity that behaves in the same way—though of course not on the same spectrum—as electromagnetism?

Typical of such researchers are Dr. Joseph Weber whose paper entitled, "Evidence for Discovery of Gravitational Radiation" was published in 1969; Harold L. Davis's treatise, "Gravity Pulses Confirmed—But Where Do They Come From?"; and two active researchers in this theory, Ramon Bisque and George Rouse who teamed to present their joint study in a work called, "Geoid and Magnetic Field anomalies; Their Relationship to the Core-Mantle Interface" in 1968.

It is interesting to note here a fact the high school student of physics learns: the magnetic compass doesn't normally point to the true north, but to the "magnetic north." Mariners and pilots refer to this as "compass variation." As a sailor or flyer circumnavigates the earth, this variation changes. In some places it amounts to as much as 20 degrees. The navigator must always compensate for this compass error or he will find himself far from where he thinks he is.

But here we can pause to note a most interesting aspect of this magnetic attraction: there are two places on our globe where the compass *does* point to true north. One spot is the Bermuda Triangle and the other the Devil's Sea area!

Is there a relationship here between these compass rarity zones and the disappearances? An especially thought-provoking consideration when one recalls the many instances of pilots just prior to their vanishing, reporting a feeling of being *confused as to direction*. Does some magnetic aberration occur that affects the normal compass determinations?

Remember one such typical example in the reply from Lt. Charles Taylor on Flight 19, the "Lost Patrol" when the radio tower asked him his position?

"We are not sure . . . We seem to be lost . . ."

Then a few minutes later, "We cannot be sure which way is west . . . everything is wrong . . . strange . . . we cannot be sure of any direction . . ."

Or could this sense of confusion be related

not to compasses or magnetism at all but, as some investigators contend, to a disorientation in man's own mind?

An example of this could well be the pilot of the private plane attempting a landing at Nassau in the Bahamas as we have mentioned earlier, who, although it was a perfectly fair day enabling him to see clearly without need of instrument aid, pleaded for guidance from the control tower as though he were "descending in a pea-soup fog!"

Such a disorientation, suggest some researchers, could be caused by the strange effect of some kind of unknown electromagnetic force.

Studies in the possible anomalies that might be occurring in electromagnetic forces are being carried on by researching scientists today that may ultimately aid in getting to the bottom of the Triangle Mystery. More and more, articles in scientific magazines are appearing on this subject (pieces like the item by George D. Curtis published in *Undersea Technology* on August 1964, "An Electromagnetic Radiation Pattern Over the Ocean.")

In the words of a Navy interviewee spoken to a reporter a few years ago on this subject:

"It's all been a real mystery. Nobody in the Navy sneers at this thing. We've always known there's something strange about this Bermuda Triangle. There doesn't seem to be any logical explanation. It's almost as though craft of every kind become suddenly covered by some sort of electronic camouflage net."

Navy pilots, commercial pilots, in fact, flyers from every walk of life, have their own private views on the Bermuda Triangle Mystery. And *private*, they really are and, according to many pilot interviewees, *private* they must remain.

As one typical commercial flyer related it to a journalist a few years ago,

"A lot of pilots have seen strange things they can't explain but they're afraid to talk about them or report them. It might cost them their jobs."

What are the theories of the pilots, by and large?

"Well," many a flyer will tell you, "one of the most frequently expressed speculations is that of an unstable aberration in the atmosphere."

What kind of aberration?

"Who can say? Maybe a hole in the sky or a force that throws them into another time dimension?"

But, of course, it must be stated here, officially the Navy refutes any such theory as to an atmospheric aberration. There is not sufficient evidence, the department points out, to support it.

However, the possibility of anomalies in time is absorbing man's investigative mind. Not only have the impending victims of the Bermuda Triangle made final feverish implications in certain cases that they were confused as to direction, but many made it clear that they were confused as to *time*, as well as *direction*, as when the Lost Patrol stated: "Everything seems wrong."

On many occasions, in many parts of the world, over the years, airplanes have been offering possible evidence of time irregularities.

On courses over the Polar regions, this is fairly common. Flyers have long implied that there is "something wrong with time" in those areas. That there is something "wrong" or deviant from the regular rule, as to direction has long been alleged to exist at the North Pole. Men crossing the ice on sleds or on foot have reported for well over a century a complete "turning around" of their direction estimates because of the fact that compasses are highly unreliable and won't work at all for weeks at a stretch because of the gravitic and magnetic peculiarities of the Polar region.

It's a well known fact that it is difficult even to take a "reading" from a star because the Polar ice raft itself circles and drifts among its floes. Even modern scientists with the most sophisticated instruments have found it a problem to ascertain where they are or how far they must go. All of which corroborates the old hue and cry of yesteryear's explorers who complained on their expeditions that they were not as far as they wished; or they had gone too far. Or they felt they had traveled too fast or too slow.

Modern Arctic expeditions have met with orientation peculiarities. Researchers like Massachusetts scientist, Tom Sexton, who once spent months on an ice mass, tell of the strange phenomenon of "whiteout." In wide expanses of snow and ice, the eye cannot "get a bearing." A matchbox a few yards away can appear to be a tall building in the far distance.

"It's a weird experience," says Sexton. "One gets literally 'white-washed' after a length of time. Disoriented—confused. I wouldn't want to experience it again!"

Adding to the experience of explorers in the North Pole region, airplanes for some time now have been presenting evidence from other parts of the world that occasional time irregularities beyond human explanation have occurred.

Examples of such instances have been racked up principally in the Pacific around Guam. On flights in perfectly clear, star-dazzled nights, pilots have from time to time, found they arrived at their destinations so far ahead of schedule as to be unbelievable. The flight time recorded implied such a speed could only be the result of a force of a 500-mile-an-hour wind. Yet such instances occurred when there were scarcely any winds at all!

These experiences are not hearsay. They are reports from professional pilots and are supported by official flight records.

Is *Time*, then, the key to the Bermuda Triangle Mystery?

Albert Einstein theorized that Time is a fourth dimension. Man has more than Height, Width and Depth to contend with in scientific calculations, he asserted. He has Time.

Such an intriguing possibility has given food to plot-thought in science-fiction writing for centuries. Has the hour come to mankind in which the theory is to be more than story food? Is it here—upon us now—as a possible fact?

Many men are turning their examining minds in this direction today. They cannot help but do so. Too many things are occurring that push them into such considerations.

Instances like the following one, called the strangest case ever experienced by the Civil Aeronautics Board since its inception. The CAB was not able to produce a common sense solution, it is said, though it pored over a file cabinet-full of evidence for months—all of which supported every word the flyer told of his experience.

The story concerns the pilot of a private plane in 1961. He was flying alone in the skies over Ohio, sweeping past great creamy clouds when, suddenly, pulling out of a misty puff he found that he was right on top of another plane!

Startled, the pilot banked swiftly but not quick enough to avoid striking the other plane with one silver wing-tip. Righting himself and flying straight on, the pilot swallowed his heart that had jumped into his throat and looked back. He had to check out what he had seen. He saw that he was right. He had averted a near fatal mid-air crash with an oldtime plane! It was a biplane of pre-World War 1 vintage constructed of wood and canvas. The pilot was as old-fashioned looking as the plane—he was wearing a leather flying helmet and wide goggles.

In the next moment, the old plane with its fine-wire struts curved into a cloud and was gone from sight.

The pilot zoomed home as fast as he could make it, landed with his heart still pounding and hurried to fill out a report. Some damn fool in a patched-up-craft was up there wreaking havoc! He'd like to wring his neck!

To his astonishment, the flyer found after careful search that there was no such plane on record anywhere flying about in the area. No airfield in the state or nearby had any such plane in their environs. The pilot even searched the lists of licenses. There had been none issued to such a craft.

Checking out crash possibilities in that section of the country, he found that not one had occurred anywhere near the time he spotted the old plane.

Unbelieving, the flyer shook his head and chalked up his experience as the weird wonder of his life.

Then, a few months later the man heard of an astounding thing: a plane just like the one he described encountering was found not far away in a barn covered with a pile of hay! It was determined by experts who examined the craft that it had been in that position, untouched, for many years.

But there was still more to be unearthed! In the pilot's pouch was found a log book. In the last entry the pilot noted a harrowing experience he'd just had. While flying through the clouds that morning, he had suddenly come upon another plane—a "large silver aeroplane" that collided with him! Fortunately it had just scraped him with its wing tip not doing enough damage to cripple him. Then the shining plane pulled away and was gone. The pilot had been badly scared and gave profound thanks for being alive.

The Ohio pilot was stunned by the discovery. The old book was turned over to the CAB, according to the story, who, in turn, ran tests on it and the results confounded the aeronautical agency who was sure the whole thing was a hoax.

But was it? The log book checked out as being authentic and the entry nearly fifty years old!

After this amazing announcement, the CAB, reputedly, had the oldtime craft carefully gone over and checked for evidence. What did they find? A long scrape mark the length of one side with traces of paint and aluminum. Those traces of substance were put through laboratory tests and found to match up perfectly with the material of the modern plane!

In spite of such conclusions, the CAB, we are told, stuck firm to its conviction that, no matter what, it had to be a hoax. Those who knew the pilot testified to his integrity and sincerity. He was not the "hoax type." Yet, what else could such an incident be attributed to?

Perhaps to a Time anomaly? Can people move back in time—or forward for a moment? Classic cases of such experiences have occurred over the years and are still happening. Take a place like Versailles. From time to time for over a century, certain persons have experienced "stepping back in time" for a brief time. As recently as 1972 a couple from Doylestown, Pennsylvania, were visting Versailles with a crowd of tourists. There must have been a flow of a hundred people pouring towards the palace entrance. Suddenly, Mr. and Mrs. Joseph Frazer looked over to the right of them. It was just in time to catch sight of a young girl in 17th century dress with a cap on her head, coming out of a side door and disappearing through another one a few yards beyond. She appeared to be a serving girl.

The couple found by inquiring that no such costumed girl was on the grounds, nor were the doors in question in use. They were locked and unused and had been for a long, long time.

What had happened? Did the Frazers slip back in time, as perhaps, did the Ohio pilot? Is this possible Time aberration related to the

Bermuda Triangle disappearances? Did everybody step back in time? Or did they plunge forward in time? Are they in another dimension?

Dr. Manson Valentine, Ph.D., the much-respected explorer into the Bahama Islands past, is well known for his investigations of what is considered to be the ruins of a sunken city in those islands. He expressed an opinion to an inquiring reporter a few years ago relating to the Bermuda Triangle Mystery. What happened to everybody?

"They are all still here, in a different time dimension," the scientist replied.

How did they get into such a dimension?

"As the result of a magnetic phenomenon."

And what might be the basis of such a magnetic aberration?

"It could be set up by a UFO."

And there we have another conjecture. Are UFO's or Spaceships or Men from Outer Space a part of the Triangle Mystery?

Many serious-minded and thoughtful individuals, scientists and laymen alike, declare that they are.

John Wallace Spencer, author and lecturer, stated on a recent Talk Show with Joel Spivak on WCAU-Radio in Philadelphia that he believed a space ship larger than the Empire State building descends periodically to pick up men, ships and planes to take back to a home planet for study.

Thousands of UFO devotees support Spencer in this theory. The Bermuda Triangle is a "Collecting Basin" for visitors from Outer Space.

Other UFO enthusiasts like Ted Owens, the well-known American psychic, have gone so far as to predict that a wave of UFO's will "issue forth" from both the Bermuda Triangle and the Devil's Triangle in the Pacific to prove to skeptics that Flying Saucers and the Men from Outer Space that man them, really do exist.

Owens should know, he feels, for he, himself, has been chosen by Space Intelligences to be their mouthpiece here on Earth. He declares he is being used by SI's to contact people of this world and warn them of what is going to happen.

Then there is the opposite direction to consider. The late Ivan Sanderson, scientist, editor and author, stated on a WCAU show that he believed there are civilizations under the oceans of the world. Life not only began in the water, he declared, but has, in some cases, remained there. And from time to time, these beings of superior intelligence, pluck down to their abodes for examination, samples of earth's men and ships of today.

There seems to be no end to the expansion of thought today in theorizing about the Bermuda Triangle Mystery. And, perhaps, that is the golden side of the coin, so long buried in the silt of neglect.

For it is in expanding thought, nearly everyone agrees, that the answer to everything lies.

Recently, Paul Stevens Basile, an engineer involved in research work on the space shuttle flight control system of NASA's space program, made comments that sum up the attitudes man is moving forwards with today in his study of the Unknown.

"The great 'practical' problems of man's existence have always been solved by expanding thought," he declares. "Look at man's past challenges and how he met them. 'Absolute' laws of science stated that the world was flat. Men like Columbus refused to accept that limited thinking. Throughout following centuries 'absolute' laws dictated that buildings could not stand without pillars for support; iron and steel machines could not possibly fly; sound and pictures could never travel through wires.

"Where would we be today if man had stayed within the limits of such thinking? Nowhere. Progress would have ceased."

So man has learned by experience that 'absolute' laws are not absolute at all but relative, Basile tells us. When so-called "laws" are challenged by those whose thoughts have gone beyond a presently-accepted limitation, such "laws" change. And they always will, we are assured.

What about today's "absolutes?" Such "facts" that travel to the stars is impossible because it would take centuries? Or moving through Time is sheer fantasy?

"These facts basing such statements," asserts Basile, "are relative. They can give way any time to new, expansive concepts. We will travel both to the stars and through Time, just as soon as thought expands that far. Just as no 'absolute law' of a flat earth kept 15th century men confined to Europe but their own limited thinking did, so the distance to the stars does not confine man to Earth today, but his belief in a finite speed does."

What a lot to think on!

Is the Bermuda Triangle Mystery man's greatest and most recent challenge? Will it prove to be his most workable "workshop"—a place in which to grow the fastest and farthest in his thinking and experience?

THE END